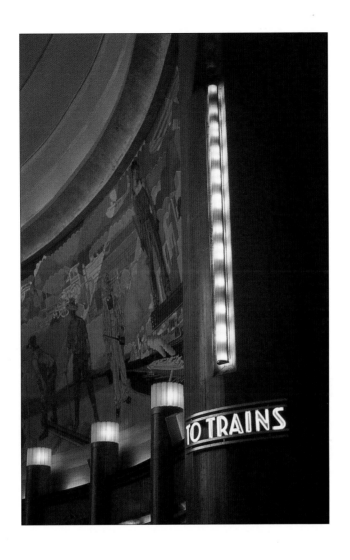

CLASSIC AMERICAN
RAILROAD
TERMINALS

KEVIN J. HOLLAND

MBI Publishing Company

Acknowledgments

Tangible proof that railroad stations—the grand and not-so-grand—were a cornerstone of North American life through the first half of the twentieth century survives in the form of postcards. These pocket-sized manifestations of civic and corporate pride depicted their subjects for all the world to see—and today they provide a remarkable and colorful opportunity to look back upon a time and a way of life which have largely vanished.

Postcards were, in many ways, the e-mail of their day, and it is therefore fitting that I should trace my involvement in a book relying heavily on vintage postcard images to an innocuous e-mail message. Paul D. Schneider made that fateful correspondence possible, and for that I am grateful.

As remarkable a record as they are, postcards can be, nonetheless, rather idealized and sometimes even surreal depictions of their subject—they were, after all, produced as a form of advertising. Photographs offer a more definitive form of visual documentation, and many of the terminals on the pages that follow are also seen through the eyes of these talented and sensitive photographers: Dick Acton Sr., Jim Boyd, Alan Bradley, Bob Bullermann, Peter Carroll, Richard J. Cook Sr., John Dziobko, Bruce Fales, John Gruber, Robert Hale, Jim Heuer, Joe Greenstein, A.M. Langley Jr., Mark Llanuza, Alex Mayes, Mike McBride, M.D. McCarter, Robert T. McCoy, Joe McMillan, George Melvin, Jim Neubauer, Otto Perry, Howard Robins, Mike Schafer, Jim Scribbins, Jim Shaughnessy, and Brian Solomon. Following "the road less traveled," these photographers have documented structures which, even in their prime, were largely taken for granted.

I am grateful as well to Mark Harland Johnson for granting permission to reproduce his painting of Jacksonville Terminal on pages 98–99. Ed Birch, Phil and Bev Birk, John B. Corns, Kevin T. Farrell, Dave Ingles, Bob Liljestrand, Nate Molldrem, Al Paterson, David Shaw, Bob Stanley, Jim Starosta, Kim Tschudy, Joe Welsh, Jay Williams, and Bruce Young generously shared photographs and other items from their collections, as did the Allen County (Ohio) Historical Society, the Chesapeake & Ohio Historical Society, the Canada Science & Technology Museum, Cleveland State University, the Denver Public Library, the Detroit Photographic Company Collection of the Library of Congress, the Milwaukee Road Historical Association, the New Orleans Public Library, Railroad Avenue Enterprises, the University of Massachusetts-Lowell/B&M Archives, and the University of Southern California.

Historical material on still-active terminals was provided by Amtrak, Canadian Pacific, GO Transit (Toronto), MARC (Washington, D.C.), MBTA (Boston), Metra (Chicago), Metrolink (Los Angeles), Metro-North Railroad (New York), NJ Transit (Hoboken), SEPTA (Philadelphia), and Sound Transit (Seattle).

Insight into redeveloped terminal properties came from material furnished by the Chattanooga Choo Choo, the Museum Center at Union Terminal (Cincinnati), the Prime Osborn III Convention Center (Jacksonville), Science City at Union Station (Kansas City), the Science Museum of Virginia (Richmond), and the Western Heritage Museum (Omaha). David Lustig and Mike Tisdale helped track down film credits of some well-known terminals. Together with Mike Schafer, Steve Esposito, and Tanya Anderson of Andover Junction Publications, these individuals and institutions have made this book possible.

To Mike Schafer as well goes the credit for the book's elegant design, and my thanks for his willingness to let me meddle in it. Working on this project and watching the chapters come to life has been a particularly rewarding experience, the latest in a series set in motion by Mike—unknown to him and to me—over a dozen years ago.

—*Kevin J. Holland*

To Graeme and Russell

First published in 2001 by MBI Publishing, 729 Prospect Avenue, PO Box 1, Osceola, WI 54020

© Andover Junction Publications, 2001

Editing and book design by Mike Schafer; layout by Mike Schafer and Tanya Anderson, Andover Junction Publications, Lee, Illinois, and Blairstown, New Jersey.

Front cover: Heralded as one of the most beautiful railroad terminals ever built, Cincinnati Union Terminal glows on an August evening in 1998. The Art Deco wonder opened at the onset of the Great Depression. The station fell on hard times in the 1970s after the last passenger train departed; it survived ludicrous proposals to have it completely razed (part of it was) and was magnificently reborn in the 1990s as a multi-use facility, including—again—as a passenger-train station. *Mike Schafer*

Frontispiece: Subtle signage amidst the breathtaking Art Deco splendor of Cincinnati Union Terminal points travelers to their steel-wheeled conveyances. *Mike Schafer*

Title page: The restored grandeur of Union Station greets travelers visiting Washington, D.C., in March 2000. *Alex Mayes*

Contents page: For decades, *the* meeting place in Manhattan has been at the information clock of New York's Grand Central Terminal, shown in 1999. *Joe Greenstein*

Foreword page: Cathedral or railroad terminal? A trio of nuns approach the Canal Street entrance to Chicago Union Station's head house in 1964. *John Gruber*

Endpapers: Synonymous with hustle and bustle, New York's Grand Central Terminal is easily the most well-recognized railroad terminal in America. This postcard scene dating from the time of the depot's unveiling early in the twentieth century also mirrors how GCT appears today, following a mutli-million-dollar restoration in the 1990s. *Mike Schafer collection*

Back cover: A passenger for New Jersey Transit obtains ticketing for her commuter-train journey west from NJT's crown jewel depot, Hoboken Terminal, in 1981. Since its opening in 1907, Hoboken Terminal has continuously served as a gateway to New York City on the opposite shore of the Hudson River via ferry boats and subways that serve the home of the erstwhile Lackawanna Railroad. *Mike Schafer*

Library of Congress Cataloging-in-Publication Data
ISBN 0-7603-0832-2

Printed in China

CONTENTS

FOREWORD

Ever since I laid eyes upon photographer John Gruber's wonderful black-and-white image of three nuns among the colonnades of Chicago Union Station in *Trains* Magazine in the 1960s, my views on great railroad terminals took on whole new light. Railroad terminals weren't just a great gathering place for passenger trains—they were also a kind of spiritual intersection for a vast spectrum of society.

My first encounter with a major railroad terminal was Central Station in Chicago. As a four-year-old, I was awed by the cavernous waiting room and the mysterious rumblings of locomotives and trains from underneath. (With every rumbling, my sister and I would excitedly ask our mother, "Is that our train home to Rockford?") Nearly a dozen years later, I would make my first visit to Chicago Union Station, arriving from Davis Junction, Illinois, on a tardy Milwaukee Road *Arrow*. However, the four of us high-school travelers didn't have time to ponder CUS's looming columns and vaulted-ceiling concourse. We had to make a mad dash for La Salle Street Station to catch the Rock Island for Joliet Union Station. As an itinerant train-watcher and rail traveler, railroad terminals had become a regular part of my life—and, I'm happy to say, they still are.

Author Kevin Holland's work—and those of the myriad of photographers represented herein—invokes the wonder and inspiration of railway terminals and at the same time provides fascinating insight as to their creation.
—*Mike Schafer*
Lee, Illinois

"When I was a young man, I used to go to train stations and watch people and wonder what they were doing, where they were going, and I always felt better when I walked out than when I walked in. I'll bet nearly everybody here has had a similar experience."

—Former President Bill Clinton, in remarks during the launch of the Penn Station Redevelopment Project, New York, May 19, 1999.

INTRODUCTION

As the twentieth century drew to a close, North America's great railroad terminals were winning the struggle to rebound from the depths of public indifference, where they had languished with uncertain futures three or four decades earlier. Shining examples in cities as diverse as Washington, D.C., and Los Angeles had reprised their original roles as thriving gateways of transport and commerce, while troubled counterparts in Buffalo and Detroit were caught in a perilous limbo and continued to face bleak prospects for redevelopment.

Examples in the likes of Kansas City, Cincinnati, Omaha, and Richmond, Virginia, were embraced in second careers by generations who never knew them in their original guises. For each survivor, though, dozens of these once-indispensible structures had been lost to decay, urban renewal, tax avoidance, redundancy, and that most nebulous pursuit, progress.

An old adage insists, "the more things change, the more they stay the same." In the course of this book's production, I was reminded of that as I found myself spending most of a day at Chicago's O'Hare International Airport—the involuntary "guest" of a major American airline. Resigning myself to a succession of flight cancellations, two thoughts occurred to me: first (and most obvious), I should have taken the train this time; and second, air terminals and railroad terminals aren't really all that different.

As I watched the ebb and flow of humanity at O'Hare, I couldn't help but dwell on the similarities to the classic railroad terminals that airports like O'Hare had helped eradicate. In the earliest days of commercial air travel these similarities were particularly hard to miss—there even was a Grand Central Air Terminal. Presaging the hybrid Mission/Art Deco architecture of Los Angeles Union Passenger Terminal by more than a decade, it opened in Glendale, California, in 1928. The real Grand Central, in its most recent incarnation, was only 15 years old at the time and, like most teenagers, seemed immortal.

Air terminals and railroad terminals shared the necessity to channel large numbers of people in a predictable and efficient manner, and therefore exhibited commonalities in their interior layouts of ticketing, baggage, waiting, concourse, and gate areas. Today's typical air traveler would feel oddly at home in one of North America's classic rail terminals, in spite of the overwhelming likelihood that they have never set foot in one. The displaced flyer, transported back to the rail terminals' heyday, would intuitively know where to find a meal, a haircut, and a newspaper before proceeding through a teeming concourse to their appointed gate. The more things change, the more they really do stay the same.

Where the classic railroad terminals stand apart, though, is in the richness and individuality of their architecture—examples like Eero Saarinen's TWA terminal at New York's Idlewild Airport (today's JFK) and his Dulles Airport terminal in northern Virginia notwithstanding. Designers of air terminals too often have tended toward sterile caricatures as allegories for progress, a misfortune also inflicted upon those few North American railroad terminals built after World War II in cities like Toledo, Ohio; Milwaukee, Wisconsin; and Ottawa, Ontario.

This book is, admittedly, a selective and rather subjective look at some of North America's significant railroad stations ... and "significant," as readers will discover, does not necessarily always translate as "big" or "famous." True, you'll find some icons in the pages that follow—gems across the architectural spectrum ranging from New York's Grand Central Terminal to Cincinnati's Union Terminal and Los Angeles' Union Passenger Terminal.

Beyond a round-up of these and other "usual suspects," though, are included a selection of relatively unsung classics. These were the workaday terminals—tucked away from the limelight of the largest cities or overshadowed by better-known and better-patronized neighbors—that nonetheless played important supporting roles in linking the North American passenger rail system.

Since a look at railroad stations should, I think, reasonably dwell as much with railroads as it is does architecture, many of the photographs on the following pages present these classic terminals from the perspective of their *raison d'etre* ... the trains themselves, and their passengers. From limiteds to locals, these trains were the threads that bound North America until the traveling public's inevitable affinity for automobiles and airplanes caused them to fray.

—*Kevin J. Holland*
Burlington, Ontario

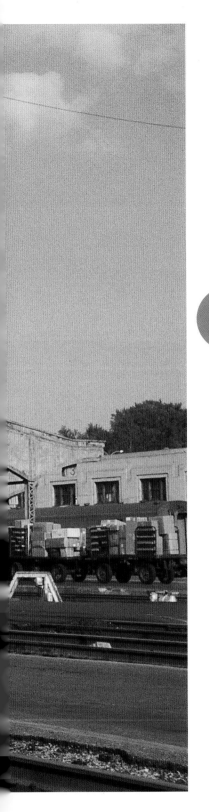

1 STYLE AND SUBSTANCE

WHAT MAKES A RAILROAD TERMINAL?

In its most basic function, a railroad station is a gateway to the village, town, or city in which it stands. A station can be as minimalistic as a sign on a post and a simple cinder platform, without the comfort of even a rudimentary depot building. Beyond that, there is the archetypal—and largely vanished—small-town depot, often just a simple one- or two-story wood-frame or brick structure adjacent to a branch or main line. "Down at the depot," the railroad's local agent would ensure that his or her employer's operations ran smoothly, while serving as an invariably congenial host for passengers, local shippers, and neighborhood kids alike.

At the other end of the spectrum, most often associated with major cities, was the railroad terminal. These often took the form of an awe-inspiring, lofty building with a wondrous assortment of tracks, platforms, and trains.

Much like today's JFK or O'Hare International Airports, railroad passenger terminals were once *the* gateways for major cities. As such, it was important that these stations reflected the spirit and personality of the cities they served, all the while serving passengers as efficiently as feasible.

ABOVE: Rusticated granite and sandstone, soaring clock towers, and abundant arches were all hallmarks of an architectural style pioneered by H.H. Richardson in the late nineteenth century. His widely emulated expression of what he termed the "masculinity" of public buildings such as courthouses and prisons found favor with railroads, resulting in Richardsonian Romanesque structures like Indianapolis Union Station, shown in 1971.—JIM HEUER

LEFT: Kansas City Union Station—where Santa Fe's westbound *Chief*, *Kansas Cityan*, and *Tulsan* (left to right) posed in mid-1965—exemplified the Beaux Arts "revolution" in public architecture that occurred following the 1893 World's Columbian Exposition in Chicago. Neo-classical themes prevailed in railroad terminal architecture through the 1920s, when the emergence of the Art Deco movement signaled another shift in public tastes.—MIKE MC BRIDE

"Stub" versus "through" terminals: In stub-end terminal arrangements, the tracks literally end within the station confines. This scene of Burlington Northern's *California Zephyr* loading at Chicago Union Station—during the three weeks in March 1970 when the BN and *CZ* co-existed—shows the stub-end arrangement, with the rear of the train backed to the end of track (the "bumping post"). Usually nearby is a track gate sign indicating the train, its name and number, the track on which it is boarding, and the car locations within the train's "consist" or car arrangement.—MIKE MC BRIDE

A postcard view of Union Station at Burlington, Vermont, shows a common through-track arrangement for larger-city terminals. As the name implies, non-terminating trains can make their passenger stop and then continue. Note integration of concourse above tracks.—MIKE SCHAFER COLLECTION

What makes a railroad station a "terminal?" There is a degree of latitude—and a bit of Latin—in the definition, with the common bond involving a station facility where some trains, but not necessarily all, originate or terminate. *Webster's* succinctly confirms the composite nature of a terminal as a "passenger station that is central to a considerable area or serves as a junction at any point with other lines."

New York's Pennsylvania Station and Toronto's Union Station, for example, both straddled through-track layouts, yet from the passengers' perspective the majority of their trains operated as if the tracks were stub-ended. Seattle Union Station was a textbook stub-end terminal yet, as far as the Milwaukee Road was concerned, in function it was an admittedly awkward through station. Even St. Louis Union Station, a classic—and mammoth—stub-end design, hosted the occasional through train. Stations found in smaller cities like Chattanooga, New Orleans, and Detroit were classic stub-end terminals, demonstrating that sheer size does not make a station a terminal, nor does track layout in and of itself. Examples like these broaden—and blur—the definition of a terminal beyond the traditional urban landmarks.

Whatever their physical size or track layout, terminal stations are most consistently defined by the presence of "housekeeping" services catering to their terminating and originating trains. Coach yards, commissaries, car washers, and laundry services—humming with activity as passenger cars were cleaned and restocked between the conclusion of one trip and the beginning of the next—were vital to a terminal's daily functioning. Lineside depots, serving trains only during typically brief stops, had little need for such facilities beyond "watering" or "icing" cars en route.

Locomotives, too, had their servicing needs fulfilled adjacent to the "textbook" terminal. The roundhouses, turntables, water tanks, and coaling docks of the steam era may have given way to the less-demanding service needs of the diesel locomotive, but the need for maintenance and replenishment of fuel and water between runs remained.

The larger a terminal was, the more complex its trackwork was sure to be—and the greater the need for outlying interlocking towers to control track switches, signaling, and train movements. Generally two- or three-story affairs adjacent to a terminal's throat and approach trackage, these towers performed vital traffic-control functions analogous to their present-day airport counterparts.

TERMINAL COMPONENTS

The terminology applied to terminals reveals many titles whose meanings are obvious, along with a few less so. Typically, a railroad terminal's most immediate functions—from the perspective of a passenger embarking on a journey—were grouped about a large, high-ceilinged "signature" space variously referred to as a Great Hall,

Grand Lobby, Main Hall, Ticket Hall, Main Waiting Room, or similarly impressive title. Here, passengers could expect to find ticket windows, baggage and parcel check rooms, an information kiosk, telephones, washrooms, Redcap service, and other necessities of departure. For their part, arriving passengers knew this was where they could secure rubber-tired transportation to conclude their journeys.

With their tickets and baggage attended to, travelers were typically offered a choice of eating establishments adjacent to the station's largest hall, ranging from a Fred Harvey or Union News Company dining room or lunch counter to cocktail lounges and, in later years, the ubiquitous snack bar. Ancillaries such as newsstands and barber shops were also found adjacent to the main hall.

"Waiting Room" seems a simple enough term, but it became somewhat more complicated in actual practice. Stations catering to large volumes of long-distance passengers and connecting trains were obliged to provide appropriately large waiting areas, while terminals with predominant commuter traffic did not have the same burden. Sometimes, as we have seen, the main hall doubled as a primary waiting area, in which a large number of seats—usually unforgiving wooden benches—were provided. In fact, multiple waiting rooms were originally provided in just about every North American railroad terminal, with separate facilities for women, male smokers, immigrants, and, in the case of the "Jim Crow" South, African-Americans.

One of the more nebulous terminal terms was "concourse," which, generally, referred to a transition space between the waiting areas and the trains themselves. In some terminals, most notably Boston's South Station and St. Louis Union Station, this gathering area was referred to as the "Midway" and was originally open to the sights, sounds, and smells of the train shed. In the case of New York's Grand Central Terminal, the main hall doubled as the concourse for long-distance passengers, whose waiting rooms were located elsewhere. Montreal's Central Station and Philadelphia's Thirtieth Street Station, both built entirely over their tracks, managed to combine just about every important long-distance function, from ticketing to train gates, into one main hall. Some terminals, like Toronto Union Station, incorporated separate arrival and departure concourses.

ABOVE: **The ticketing area of Chicago Union Station before the building was drastically altered beginning in the late 1960s. This area was located in the under-street portion of Union Station connecting the concourse building with the head house.**—JIM HEUER

LEFT: **Coach yards were a must for terminals. This is a 1972 view of Illinois Central's Weldon Coach Yard, located immediately south of Chicago's Central Station and west of Soldier Field (background). Here, as with nearly all coach yards, diners and lounge cars were restocked and all cars cleaned and serviced, inside and out, between runs. Yard structures warehoused frequently replaced car parts such as window glass and seating components, and provided storage of china, silverware, linens, and restroom supplies.**—MIKE SCHAFER

ABOVE: Passengers boarding Chesapeake & Ohio's *George Washington* don't need the train shed's protection from the weather on this nice afternoon in Louisville, Kentucky, in 1965. This type of shed was common on both through and stub-end terminals built in the late nineteenth century in medium-size cities east of the Missouri River. Note the roof clerestory for venting smoke and exhaust. Similar train sheds could be found in Milwaukee, Wisconsin; Grand Rapids, Michigan; Montgomery, Alabama; Portland, Maine; Augusta, Georgia; Minneapolis, Minnesota; and Nashville, Tennessee.—JIM BOYD

RIGHT: The main entrance to Indianapolis Union Station, 1971. Trains of the Pennsylvania, Big Four Route (New York Central), Monon, Baltimore & Ohio, and Illinois Central once called at this Richardsonian Romanesque facility, designed by Thomas Rodd and opened in 1888 to replace America's first true "union" station. The Art Deco marquee was a 1930s addition.—MIKE SCHAFER

The typical concourse, more aptly described as a "train concourse," was effectively an enclosed annex of the main station structure (the "head house"). Limited waiting space was usually provided in the concourse, where departing passengers congregated to present their tickets at gates leading to track level. In through terminals, the concourse was built perpendicular to the track orientation, crossing either above the tracks (as in Cincinnati, Dallas, Buffalo, Kansas City, and others) or below (as at Toronto, Detroit, and Winnipeg). In stub-end layouts, the concourse was placed between the head house and end-of-track bumpers, eliminating stairs and ramps but ensuring a lengthy walk for at least some passengers.

Having progressed to track level, passengers (and station personnel) were usually protected from the elements by structures ranging from simple platform canopies to elaborate train sheds. The earliest such sheds were mammoth arched structures, often referred to as "balloon sheds." They kept most of the weather out, but kept in smoke, soot, and other noxious by-products of the trains' steam and diesel-electric locomotives. Pitch-roof train sheds with clerestories were popular at smaller terminals, and they allowed smoke to escape into the sky. In 1905, the Bush train shed was developed by Lackawanna Railroad Chief Engineer Lincoln Bush. The design's low profile and efficient track-center ventilation made it and its derivatives popular choices for terminal planners.

UNION STATIONS

As a network of established and fledgling railroads spread west of the Appalachian Mountains toward the Mississippi in the mid-nineteenth century, towns and cities often found themselves with as many railroad stations as they had railroads. The shortcomings of this situation were quickly realized by passengers obliged to connect from one road to another, and by civic leaders faced with the track and traffic congestion of duplicative stations and approaches. The solution was the "union" station, as envisioned by General Thomas Armstrong and first executed at Indianapolis in 1853.

Union Depot, Detroit, Mich.

Detroit's Fort Street Union Depot, opened in 1893, illustrates the Richardsonian Romanesque style, though office space had enlarged the cross-section of what was usually a slender clock tower on such buildings. The Pere Marquette, Wabash, and Pennsylvania railroads owned the stub-ended terminal through their jointly held subsidiary, the Union Belt Railroad of Detroit. The Chesapeake & Ohio, having acquired the Pere Marquette through merger in 1947, went on to become Fort Street's sole owner in the terminal's last years. Horse-drawn carriages and, later, automobiles and trucks were spared the delays and hazards of crossing the terminal's approach tracks, which were elevated above street level for a distance of 15 blocks from the head house.—KEVIN HOLLAND COLLECTION

Predicated on the ability of railroads—often rivals competing for the same traffic—to cooperate, the benefits of a union station to passengers, municipalities, and the railroads themselves were obvious and immediate. Connecting passengers no longer had to endure transfers between multiple stations. Civic leaders saw what was often a smothering carpet of competing station approach trackage reduced to one shared route. Consolidations of this sort reduced the number of dangerous grade crossings and could eliminate them altogether when the new approach routes were elevated. For the price of cooperation—typically under the guise of a joint subsidiary terminal company—the railroads were spared the financial burden of staffing, maintaining, and paying taxes on their own individual terminal properties. This, and the convenience to passengers, overrode the rivalry factor between competing railroads serving the same city.

STATION ARCHITECTURE

The architectural evolution of the North American railroad terminal after about 1880 can be broadly summarized within three distinct and progressive phases. The Romanesque Revival style as popularized by architect Henry Hobson Richardson—with its dark, rusticated stonework, tall clock towers, steeply pitched roofs, and trademark arched entranceways—was very much in vogue with the public and station architects alike until the last

decade of the nineteenth century. Richardson drew his inspiration from elements of medieval Italian and Spanish architecture, and even after his death in 1886 his emulators perpetuated the style in railroad terminal applications throughout the East, Midwest, and Northwest.

The World's Columbian Exposition of 1893 in Chicago had an abrupt and profound impact on the design of public buildings in North America, and its neoclassical legacy was seen in new railroad terminal construction for the better part of three decades—at the rather sudden expense of the Richardsonian Romanesque. The "White City," as the Court of Honor pavilions at the 1893 Exposition came to be known, was the first major manifestation of the "City Beautiful" Movement championed by Chicago architect Daniel Burnham. Rather paternalistically, the Movement sought to renew and revitalize America's increasingly industrialized and polluted cities, inspiring their citizens through what was termed "the gospel of beauty"—the introduction of classically styled public buildings, statuary, and formal gardens, parks, and green spaces. The White City *was* the City Beautiful—albeit temporary. Permanence came within a decade, when Burnham, landscape architect Frederick Law Olmsted, sculptor Augustus Saint-Gaudens, and architect Charles F. McKim—working together as Senator James McMillan's Commission on the Improvement of the Park System—developed and implemented plans that

Without so much as a glance, New Yorkers rush past one of the city's most-famous landmarks in 1995. Grand Central Terminal is a textbook example of the Beaux-Arts architecture which dominated railroad terminal construction early in the twentieth century. This style of head-house design fell from popularity in the 1930s, but there is newfound appreciation for its esthetics at the dawn of the new millennium.—JOE GREENSTEIN

The emergence of the Art Deco movement in the mid-1920s was reflected in station projects like Fellheimer & Wagner's 1929 Buffalo Central Terminal.—MIKE SCHAFER COLLECTION

revived Pierre L'Enfant's 1789 vision of Washington, D.C, and created today's park-like Mall and Reflecting Pool.

Among the monumental public buildings eventually erected as part of the McMillan Commission's planning was Burnham's Washington Union Station, with its styling inspired by the teachings of l'Ecole des Beaux Arts in Paris. The Beaux Arts influence would be seen in railroad terminals and other public architecture in the U.S. and Canada well into the third decade of the twentieth century. Colonnades, cavernous vaulted interior spaces, statuary, and the liberal use of light-colored marble and limestone were among the traits shared by these neo-classical Greek Revival and Italianate terminal structures. They could be found throughout North America, in major cities such as

New York, Chicago, and Kansas City, and—suitably reduced in scale—in smaller centers like Scranton, Utica, Albany, St. Paul, Dallas, Winnipeg, and Vancouver.

By the mid-1920s, new European influences were reshaping architecture and public tastes on both sides of the Atlantic, with Beaux-Arts classicism falling into outdated disfavor just as Richardsonian Romanesque had after 1893. The Exposition des Arts Decoratifs et Industriels, held in Paris in 1925, lent its abbreviated name to the new style: Art Deco. Signature elements included streamlined curvilinear forms, angular patterns of decoration, and the incorporation of exotic materials and colors in interior decor. American railroads and suppliers embraced streamlining during the 1930s— sometimes to absurd extremes—capturing the public's attention with new-generation trains like Budd's articulated *Zephyrs* and *Flying Yankee* as well as old steam locomotives masquerading under bathtub-like shrouds. For the first time, prominent industrial designers such as Raymond Loewy, Henry Dreyfus, Otto Kuhler, Walter Dorwin Teague, and Paul Cret were retained to style passenger-train paint schemes, locomotives, and interior decor. Railroad architecture also reflected the sweeping new style, with stations and terminals in Buffalo, Syracuse, Omaha, and Cincinnati among the most significant products of the Art Deco period.

As the International Style and Modern Classicism coalesced in the mid-1930s and evolved into ever more simplified and stylized derivatives of Art Deco architecture, the era of North American railroad terminal construction had, for the most part, concluded. The handful of post-Art Deco terminals—Hamilton, Ontario; Montreal, Quebec; Roanoke, Virginia: Toledo, Ohio; and New Orleans, Louisiana, among them—are rather austere end notes to the story of America's classic railroad terminals. Nonetheless, Art Deco styling has endured the decades, even enjoying a revival in the late twentieth century. When Amtrak heavily revamped Chicago Union Station's eastern half early in the 1990s, that part of the station re-emerged with a classy new "retro-Deco" look.

THE ROLE OF THE TERMINAL IN AMERICA

From today's transportation perspective, railroad terminals functioned as the international airports of their day—a community's window to the country, and the world. Comings and goings, war and peace, birth and death, commerce and leisure—all touched, and were touched by, the railroad station. Highways, airlines, television, and personal computers have all contributed to the "shrinking world," and in so doing have accelerated North Americans' break away from the railroad terminal—and the railroad itself—as a part of their daily lives.

Thousands still pass through the surviving terminals every day in cities like New York, Boston, Washington, Chicago, Toronto, and Los Angeles. For most, these classic structures are little more than a brief interlude in their daily commute—a disruption between coach seat and sidewalk, barely cause to glance up from the day's newspaper. To a few, the terminals' vaulted halls offer respite; a chance to reflect on an earlier time when commerce and permanence were synonymous, and when a railroad station's size, architecture, and location spoke volumes about the community— and the railroads—it served.

North America's classic railroad terminals represent, for good and bad, the collective egos and aspirations of the rail tycoons, politicians, architects, and the communities they represented, captured in stone, tile, glass, steel, concrete, and wood. In a transportation context—save for the handful of exceptions in the following chapters—they have been relegated to the status of footnotes by the airport and the Interstate.

As civic icons and monuments to corporate ego, railroad terminals have handed their torch—and in some cases their real estate—to the urban sports stadium. Madison Square Garden led the way atop the bowels of New York's Pennsylvania Station in the mid-1960s, and by the end of the 1990s new sports stadiums abutted or had at least partially usurped railroad terminal property in cities like New Orleans, Boston, Seattle, Toronto, and Montreal.

With rare exceptions, the great terminals were built too big and too late—products of an era when the notion of the railroads ever losing their supremacy was simply unfathomable. History, of course, proved otherwise, as North Americans' zeal for mobility and speed rendered the great passenger terminals obsolete, if not completely redundant. Some are still with us; many are not. Some teetered on the brink, only to be rescued as society belatedly embraced adaptive reuse and multimodalism—rather clinical names for common-sense concepts.

Stained-glass windows were *de riguer* on Romanesque terminal buildings of the late nineteenth century. This rose window was located above Indianapolis Union Station's main entrance. Such details survive on this classic terminal, which underwent a major renovation in the 1980s.—JIM HEUER

② EASTERN ICONS

• NEW YORK • HOBOKEN • NEWARK • BOSTON • PORTLAND
• BANGOR • WHITE RIVER JUNCTION • ST. ALBANS
• PHILADELPHIA • WASHINGTON

The Eastern U.S., and the Northeast in particular, is liberally endowed with classic railroad terminals—a legacy of the nation's oldest and most densely populated region and its utter dependence upon the railroads during the late nineteenth and early twentieth centuries. And, in no other region of the U.S. has the traditional railroad terminal survived so well performing its intended function. One only need to travel along the Northeast Corridor between Boston and Washington where, in the space of some 460 miles, travelers can experience the grandeur of no less than seven significant terminals: Boston's South Station, New York's Grand Central, Newark's Pennsylvania Station, Thirtieth Street in Philadelphia, Baltimore's Pennsylvania Station, and Washington Union Station. Further, one major terminal is in the throes of rebirth: New York's Pennsylvania Station.

Other great Northeast terminals, past and present, found homes in cities along rail routes reaching from the great

ABOVE: In the shadow of Shepley, Rutan & Coolidge's Beaux-Arts Albany Union Station, Delaware & Hudson PA-type locomotive No. 19 rubs shoulders with a Penn Central E8A (still in New York Central colors in this 1968 scene, recorded a few months after the NYC and PRR merged to create PC). The E-unit will forward cars from the D&H's recently arrived *Laurentian* south to New York City's Grand Central Terminal. Albany Union Station opened in December 1900.—JIM SHAUGHNESSY

LEFT: A meeting place without peer in a city without peer, Grand Central Terminal's spherical clock has come to symbolize one of the world's great railroad stations. As it has been since it opened in 1913, GCT's main concourse was a hive of activity on July 21, 1999.—JOE GREENSTEIN

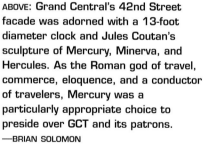

metropoli of the Atlantic coast toward the Middle West and upper New England. As the Pennsylvania Railroad, New York Central, Baltimore & Ohio, and other notable carriers marched west and northwest, great depots arose to serve them at the likes of Harrisburg, Pittsburgh, Albany, Utica, and Rochester.

NEW YORK CITY
Grand Central Terminal

It seems only fitting that New York City, as one of the world's largest and best-known cities, should boast not one but two of the busiest and most famous railroad terminals on the planet: Grand Central Terminal and Pennsylvania Station. The very name "Grand Central" remains synonymous with frenzy and bustle. Ask an American to name a railroad station—almost a trivial question in a society long enthralled by the automobile and airplane—and you'll likely have Grand Central as your quick reply. If any American railroad station qualifies as an icon, it is New York's Grand Central Terminal (GCT), described in the press while still under construction in 1911 as "the greatest railroad terminal in the world." This GCT is the second terminal to bear the name, having replaced a rebuilt predecessor on essentially the same site at 42nd Street and Park Avenue when it opened in February 1913. The complex is often mistakenly referred to as Grand Central *Station*, but

technically that moniker refers to the postal station within Grand Central Terminal.

With over 500 trains a day overtaxing the capacity of the New York Central & Hudson River Railroad's 1898 Grand Central Terminal (itself an enlargement of the original 1871 structure), a clear need existed for a new, larger facility. The 42nd Street site of the original terminal had been dictated by an 1857 city ordinance precluding steam locomotives from operating south of that cross-town artery. The issue of smoke—both as a neighborhood nuisance and an impediment to safe operation in the Park Avenue tunnel north of the terminal—further complicated matters when steam locomotives were banished completely from Manhattan under the terms of July 1903 legislation. The means of its trains' propulsion thus decreed, the railroad's planners took advantage of electrification's pollution-free nature to solve the terminal's capacity problems.

The simple solution—anywhere but in the heart of Manhattan—would have been to enlarge the terminal's capacity by enlarging its area. However, New York City land prices, even at the turn of the twentieth century, precluded this as the only option for Grand Central. Instead, New York Central's chief engineer, William Wilgus, devised a scheme to double-deck the new terminal. Long-distance trains would be accommodated on the 31-track upper level while commuter trains rode on 17 tracks below. Loop tracks on both levels reduced the need for back-up movements of trains. Electrification also solved recurring safety concerns within the terminal's Park Avenue tunnel, where smoke had been known to obscure signals with tragic results. Wilgus also recognized another strength of electrification—the trains' relative quiet and absence of pollution meant that commercial and residential structures could be built over the tracks, taking advantage of "air rights" and providing lucrative income to offset the costs of the new terminal. Accordingly, approval was secured in 1903 from the city's Board of Estimate and Apportionment to locate both terminal track levels and approach trackage in a massive excavation, which had the added benefit of removing congestion caused by former street-level trackage. All cross streets between 45th and 56th streets were restored under the terms of the plan. Structures which ultimately exploited Wilgus' air rights included the NYC's own 1929 headquarters building, the Biltmore and Waldorf-Astoria hotels, and the 1963 Pan Am Building.

The St. Paul, Minnesota-based architectural partnership of Charles Reed (who happened to be Wilgus' brother-in-law) and Allen Stem won the 1903 commission for the design of the new terminal structure. One of the first issues to be addressed by the architects was a requirement that Park Avenue not be disrupted by the new terminal, which would lie directly in the path of the major north-south artery. Rejecting the obvious but—from the perspective of an efficient station interior layout—intrusive solution of having Park Avenue run through the new terminal, Reed & Stem instead incorporated a "circumferential plaza" which wrapped an elevated Park Avenue around the outside of the building. The St. Paul partners were subsequently joined on the project by the New York firm of Warren & Wetmore—architect Whitney Warren happened to be the cousin of NYC chairman William K. Vanderbilt. The forced collaboration, with its suggestions of nepotism on the part of both firms, was a fractious one, culminating in Warren & Wetmore gaining control of the entire project in the wake of Reed's death in 1911. The victorious partnership nonetheless incorporated much of Reed & Stem's work, particularly with regard to Reed's replacement of staircases with broad ramps to expedite passenger flow to, from, and within the terminal.

Ground had been broken in June 1903, but the enormous project took ten years to complete. Much of this time was consumed by excavation work and demolition of the old terminal and train shed—all of which had to be

Stately, rather than obtrusive, electronic arrival/ departure boards are mounted above the ticket windows in the revamped GCT's main concourse, shown in the fall of 1999.—BRIAN SOLOMON

GRAND CENTRAL TERMINAL, NEW YORK, RESTAURANT

COPR. DETROIT PUBLISHING CO.

Replete with potted palms and starched linens, GCT's dining room—today the famous Oyster Bar Restaurant—was the epitome of Edwardian elegance. The room's low ceilings resulted from its location beneath the main waiting room, off of the lower-level commuter concourse.
—MIKE SCHAFER COLLECTION

Paul Helleu's illuminated—and reversed—zodiac ceiling mural was cleaned and refurbished as part of GCT's $400-million 1990s renovation. The painting depicts the stars of the northern night sky as they appear between October and March.
—JOE GREENSTEIN

structure was faced with granite and limestone. The terminal's 42nd Street facade was surmounted by sculptor Jules Coutan's grouping of Mercury, Minerva, and Hercules about a 13-foot clock. Carved immediately beneath the statuary, as if any such indication was necessary, was the inscription GRAND CENTRAL TERMINAL.

Accessed via a shallow ramp from the main 42nd Street entrance was a 205 x 65-foot main waiting room. A second ramp led passengers into the new terminal's centerpiece, the 120 x 287-foot, 125-foot-high main concourse. This magnificent room contained ticket windows for both the NYC and New Haven railroads and was punctuated at its center by an octagonal information kiosk. The spherical four-faced brass clock above the kiosk promptly became one of the terminal's most recognizable symbols and to this day a meeting place for generations of travelers.

Soaring arched windows admitted natural light, and the image of sunbeams streaming through this glazing is also inexorably linked with Grand Central. The marble-lined concourse's highlight, though, was painter Paul Helleu's celestial ceiling mural depicting the constellations of the winter night sky—with a twist. The mural was an accurate depiction of its subject, enhanced by over 60 light bulbs representing the brightest stars, but for reasons never fully established, it was backward. Whether the star positions were reversed for esthetics or, as some sources suggest, because the artist relied on Medieval references in which such presentation was common, the blue-and-gold mural is nonetheless noteworthy in a building full of superlatives.

accomplished without a marked disruption in train operation. Three million cubic yards of fill were removed during excavation, impacting an area bounded by 42nd Street on the south, 50th Street on the north, Lexington Avenue on the east, and Vanderbilt Avenue on the west.

Warren's Beaux-Arts headhouse was opened on February 2, 1913. Measuring 301 x 673 feet, the seven-story

A second, less elaborate concourse was located below the main area, accessible by wide ramps and serving the terminal's substantial commuter traffic. Corridors throughout the new terminal were lined with retail space. Baggage and express facilities were accommodated north of the main headhouse facility, adjoining 45th Street, with track-level access provided by elevators.

If Grand Central Terminal was North America's most famous railroad station, then it was entirely fitting that it should therefore host the continent's most celebrated passenger train, Central's New York–Chicago *20th Century Limited*. During the era of the streamliner, the NYC referred to its parade of intercity passenger trains—most of which operated between Grand Central and the Midwest—as the "Great Steel Fleet." Among such highly regarded services were the *Commodore Vanderbilt*, the *Southwestern Limited, Pacemaker, Ohio State Limited,* and the *Empire State Express*. GCT also served numerous suburban schedules and a raft of intercity runs belonging to the New Haven—trains with urbane or New England-inspired names like *Merchants Limited*, the *Bankers*, the *Nathan Hale*, and the *Yankee Clipper*.

Reflecting the importance of commuter traffic in its creation, Grand Central was designed to handle as many as 100 million passengers per year. Typical volumes, though, were less than half of that figure. In a scenario that would be experienced by so many of its urban counterparts, Grand Central's passenger traffic peak of 65 million passengers occurred as World War II drew to a close.

By the time a now-financially failing NYC was forced to swallow the bitter pill of merger in 1968 with its arch-rival Pennsylvania, much of Grand Central's long-distance traffic had eroded. A new NYC management had made no secret of the fact after the late 1950s that it looked upon the road's passenger trains as a cash-draining liability. Penn Central—the 1968 merger product—had the burden of its remaining intercity passenger trains removed by Amtrak in 1971, while fiscal responsibility for Grand Central's commuter trains and the station itself was gradually assumed by state transit authorities.

After two decades of subjecting connecting passengers to a sometimes daunting crosstown transfer, Amtrak on April 7, 1991, consolidated its Manhattan terminal functions at Penn Station and moved out of GCT. Amtrak trains from Upstate New York

were rerouted via the ex-NYC West Side Freight Line on Manhattan's west side to a new connection with the erstwhile PRR station. With this move, Grand Central lost a major tenant and became a commuter-only facility under the ownership of the Metro-North commuter authority.

Recognizing the operational and esthetic value of its aging landmark, Metro-North injected over $400-million during the 1990s to restore Grand Central Terminal to much of its original glory. Real-estate encroachment and development pressure had been a recurring threat to Grand Central's very survival through the 1970s and 1980s, and Metro-North's commitment to the facility was widely

Grand Central Terminal's great rival was Pennsylvania Station, shown shortly after its 1910 completion and before it was dwarfed by new surrounding skyscrapers. The sprawling facility predated the new GCT by three years. As fate would have it, however, GCT would far outlive the "real" Pennsylvania Station.—MIKE SCHAFER COLLECTION

endorsed in a city where memories of the original Pennsylvania Station's wrenching demise after 1963 were still painfully fresh. Various plans had gnawed at Grand Central's integrity, proposing everything from a high-rise office tower above (or in place of) the head house, to a bowling alley in a proposed enclosure above the main concourse. Fortunately, sanity overruled, thanks largely to Jacqueline Kennedy Onassis, wife of the late President John F. Kennedy. As one of New York City's most famed residents, Jacqueline—a regular at the terminal's famous Oyster Bar restaurant—spearheaded a movement that led to GCT being designated a national historic landmark.

As if to repudiate the lunacy of some of the earlier proposals, the main concourse became a key beneficiary of Metro-North's restoration. A long-present and overpowering Kodak advertising display was removed, skylights were reopened, cluttering kiosks were removed from the floor area, and Paul Helleu's mirror-image Zodiac ceiling mural was cleaned and re-illuminated. Funds were also allocated to improve the station's faltering electrical and mechanical

systems, and to improve pedestrian access to areas north of the terminal. Grand Central's importance to New York, and New York's consequent appreciation of Grand Central, had been confirmed—overcoming pitfalls and perils that would rob many other North American cities of their landmark terminals.

Pennsylvania Station

The Pennsylvania Railroad billed itself, without too much hyperbole, as "The Standard Railroad of the World." From its four-track "Broad Way" main line to its hundreds of standardized, home-built steam locomotives and monumental 1930s electrification, the "Pennsy" was, for decades, America's largest railroad, and the Pennsy, consequently, did things in a big way.

Electrification of its New York-area main line gave the PRR smoke-free access to Manhattan—via tunnels under the Hudson and East Rivers—in compliance with 1903 New York City smoke-abatement ordinances. For the first time, PRR was able to out-flank its ferry-bound New Jersey neighbors and compete with arch-rival New York Central right under NYC's head-office nose.

The PRR's Manhattan terminal was designed by the firm of McKim, Mead & White. At the time of its opening on November 27, 1910, it was the largest through station in the world, completed at an overall cost of $114 million. The architects' Beaux-Arts temple was inspired, in part, by the Baths of Caracalla in Rome, and it would in turn influence railroad terminal architecture across the U.S. and Canada for more than two decades.

The three-million cubic-yard excavation necessary to accommodate Pennsylvania Station's trackwork and foundations primarily affected an area bounded by Seventh Avenue on the east, Tenth Avenue on the west, West 33rd Street to the north and West 31st Street to the south. The pink Milford granite station structure itself covered two city blocks, and featured a 35-foot-tall main entrance colonnade facing Seventh Avenue. Passengers entering here traversed a 225-foot-long retail arcade before entering the station's main waiting room, a cavernous 277 x 103-foot x 150-foot high space billed at its debut—*with* some hyperbole—as the world's largest room. In the event that this area was not large enough, additional men's and women's waiting rooms—each measuring 100 x 58 feet—were located just beyond. A similarly sized restaurant and lunch room were to be found on the opposite side of the main waiting room. Ticketing and baggage-checking facilities were also located in the main waiting room.

LEFT: "Progress." Relegated to the bowels of the new Madison Square Garden complex in the mid-1960s, Penn Station became virtually invisible from the street. Would-be passengers needed a sharp eye at the corner of 7th Ave and 32nd Street in October 1998.—JOE GREENSTEIN

BELOW: Prelude. A two-ton stone eagle on the sidewalk foretold Pennsylvania Station's ultimate fate in this November 1963 scene, taken from the same vantage point as the view at left. The eagles' removal marked the symbolic commencement of the terminal's demolition.—GEORGE MELVIN COLLECTION

According to the PRR, Pennsylvania Station's main waiting room—measuring 277 feet x 103 feet x 150 feet high—was the world's largest room in 1910. The stairs at right descended from a retail arcade connecting to the terminal's 7th Avenue entrance, while the arch at left led to the concourse.—MIKE SCHAFER COLLECTION

More stairs led from the glass-roofed concourse down to the platforms and electrified tracks in what was effectively Pennsylvania Station's train shed.—MIKE SCHAFER COLLECTION

As was the case with the rest of the structure, Pennsylvania Station's concourse was built directly over the tracks—a circumstance made possible by the trains' state-mandated electrification. Contemporary newspaper reports marveled that the concourse could comfortably hold 10,000 people. This glass-roofed, two-level steel lattice-and-stone enclosure measured 341 feet wide and 210 feet long, and provided stairway access to the 21 platform tracks below. Eight of these tracks were assigned to Long Island Rail Road trains, passengers of which were also provided with their own separate ticketing and waiting areas.

Space limitations and the rapidly increasing cost of Manhattan real estate precluded the construction of adjacent equipment storage yards and other train-service facilities. The PRR opted instead to locate its Sunnyside coach yards and locomotive terminal in the Long Island borough of Queens, reached via four new tunnels under the East River (two of which accommodated trains of PRR's LIRR subsidiary). Electrified in 1933, Sunnyside's 75-track coach yard could accommodate over 1,000 passenger cars. A corresponding pair of tunnels under the Hudson River gave trains to and from the west side of Pennsylvania Station a landfall in the New Jersey meadows on the railroad's main line to Philadelphia and Washington, D.C. Completion of the New York Connecting Railroad and its Hell Gate Bridge in 1917 gave trains of the New York, New Haven & Hartford access to Pennsylvania Station for the first time, setting the stage for through services between New England and East Coast points south of New York. The New Haven had become, quite by default, a railroad in the enviable position of serving both of Manhattan's great terminals.

The combination of commuter and mainline traffic within the terminal's location in the heart of Manhattan made Pennsylvania Station the busiest facility of its kind in North America. In the peak World War II year of 1945, when stations across the U.S. were routinely faced with passenger volumes far beyond their design, Pennsylvania Station stood head and shoulders above its counterparts by handling almost 110 million passengers.

Most passengers using Pennsylvania Station were commuters traveling on the suburban trains of the Pennsylvania or the Long Island Rail Road, but it was the named limiteds that drew the attention. Pennsylvania Station was "home" to some of the greatest limiteds of railroading, not the least of which was PRR's world-class *Broadway Limited* and its companion train, the *General*, to and from Chicago. Under the station's glass-roofed atrium concourse, passengers also rushed to board joint PRR-New Haven Washington–Boston trains like the *Senator* and *Colonial*. The Lehigh Valley Railroad's modest schedules also served the PRR terminal. For winter-weary New Yorkers, Pennsylvania Station also meant a wide choice of through trains to Southeast, relayed by the PRR between New York and Washington—

On May 10, 1962, Pennsy GG1 No. 4869 emerged into the sunlight in midtown Manhattan, just outside Pennsylvania Station. The Raymond Loewy-styled motor would lead the New Haven consist, which had originated in Boston, for the remainder of its journey to Washington Union Station.—JIM SHAUGHNESSY

sunliners like Seaboard's *Silver Meteor*, Atlantic Coast Line's *Champions*, and Southern's *Southerner*.

Pennsylvania Station's destruction in the interests of real-estate redevelopment, the plans for which were announced in 1962, was a shrill call to action for architectural and railroad preservationists. The subsequent salvation of icons like Grand Central Terminal, Cincinnati Union Terminal, and Washington Union Station is directly attributable to Penn's demise, with interested parties from across society ensuring that no other terminals meet a similar uncontested fate until all reasonable redevelopment scenarios have been exhausted.

Demolition began, somewhat symbolically, on October 28, 1963, when eight two-ton stone eagles were carefully removed from the atop the terminal. Pennsylvania Station was razed in progressive phases over a three-year period, keeping pace with construction of the $70-million sports and entertainment facility that replaced it. Penn Station's post-1963 address amounted to being the basement of the new Madison Square Garden complex, where—despite a total of six street entrances and the addition of ten escalators to and from track level—inadequate and cramped facilities placed commuters and intercity travelers' needs at odds, and a subterranean squalor prevailed.

The once-mighty Pennsylvania Railroad fell on hard times in the 1960s, with its flagship station's demise just a hint of the wracking changes to come. In February 1968, the PRR merged with nemesis NYC to form Penn Central, itself a troubled company that declared bankruptcy in June 1970. Both of Manhattan's great terminals were thus under one ownership as the era of privately operated intercity rail service drew to a close in the U.S. On May 1, 1971, Amtrak assumed responsibility for the ragged survivors of PC's intercity operations.

In April 1991, Grand Central's loss was Penn's gain when Amtrak shifted its remaining intercity schedules out of the former NYC facility. "Empire Corridor" trains from Buffalo, Albany, and intermediate points (as well as the Montreal–New York *Adirondack* and the overnight Chicago–New York *Lake Shore Limited*) diverged from their old route in the South Bronx and ran south along the Hudson

continued on page 28

Movements through Penn Station were governed by two interlocking towers. This is how the interior of the west-end tower appeared in 1991, with levers controlling track switches represented in miniature on the illuminated diagram.—MIKE SCHAFER

IN THE SHADOW OF GOTHAM

Their size and mid-town Manhattan location made Grand Central Terminal and Pennsylvania Station very attractive to passengers traveling to and from New York City. Few were more acutely aware of this than those railroads that were obliged to stop short of Manhattan, over on the west shore of the Hudson. Prisoners of geography, the best they could offer long-distance patrons was a railhead terminal in the likes of Hoboken or Jersey City, with the interruption of a scenic but time-consuming ferry trip—or, in Hoboken's case, a decidedly less-scenic subway ride—between New Jersey and Gotham.

If you were in a hurry to get New York, you took the Pennsy or the New York Central. It was that simple. If you weren't in a hurry, or had a penchant for the underdog, then railroads like the Baltimore & Ohio, the Erie, and the Delaware, Lackawanna & Western entered the picture. Indeed, there was enough fringe business to sustain these latter two as marginal Chicago–New York passenger players through the late 1950s. (In the DL&W's case, Chicago was reached via through-car connecting services over both the New York Central and the New York, Chicago & St. Louis Railroad—the "Nickel Plate Road"—west of Buffalo.)

The riverside terminals erected by the Erie in Jersey City and the DL&W in Hoboken were classics in their own right. Their size reflected their importance to—and reliance upon—commuter traffic between suburban New Jersey and Manhattan. The stations' proximity to the New Jersey piers of transatlantic steamship lines like Holland-America, Scandinavian American, and United States Lines was attractive to rail passengers making train-to-ship connections on the west shore of the Hudson. Cunard and the French Line, for their part, maintained piers on Manhattan's West Side, making Grand Central or Pennsylvania Station the logical—and suitably prestigious—destinations for rail passengers embarking on the likes of the Queen Mary or Ile de France.

Hoboken's Lackawanna Terminal was designed by Robert Murchison and Lincoln Bush (the latter the Lackawanna's chief engineer and creator of the Bush train shed) and opened on February 25, 1907. The Terminal was billed as "fireproof" in a nod to the 1905 fate of its immediate predecessor

ABOVE: Erie trains—like this commuter run on January 17, 1959—moved into Hoboken after their former Jersey City terminal closed in 1957.—JOHN DZIOBKO

RIGHT: The exterior of the Lackawanna Railroad's 1907 Hoboken Terminal, with its extensive copper cladding, was rich in Art Nouveau ornamentation. Built as a link between rail and ferry services, the terminal still fulfills that role today.—KEVIN HOLLAND COLLECTION

(which had, at any rate, already been scheduled for demolition and replacement). The largely copper-clad concrete-and-steel structure acted as a conduit for commuting New Jerseyites making their way from its 16 platform tracks to the six cross-Hudson ferry slips and, after the last ferries were retired in 1967, the alternatives of buses and subway trains. The bulk of the terminal's traffic was made up, not surprisingly, of commuters—approximately 100,000 persons passed through the building each day in the years immediately following its opening. Murchison's 100 x 100-foot waiting room was embellished with limestone and plaster walls, bronze staircase railings, and a stained-glass skylight blacked out during World War II but restored to its former glory as part of a 1981 facelift. Bush's hand was evident in the design of the concourse and ferry slip areas.

By the late 1950s, it had become a foregone conclusion that the Lackawanna and the Erie were eventually going to merge. As a result, the two roads began amalgamating some of their operations well before the union, and one of the targeted rationalizations was the consolidation of passenger facilities on the Jersey side of the Hudson. During 1956–57 Erie moved out of its Jersey City terminal and into Lackawanna's Hoboken Terminal.

After intercity rail service to Hoboken ended in 1970 under the auspices of Erie's and DL&W's 1960 successor Erie Lackawanna and the arrival of EL's last Lake Cities from Chicago, the terminal became strictly a commuter facility. The electrified multiple-unit (m.u.) trains introduced at the hand of Thomas Alva Edison in 1930–31 soldiered into the early 1980s, to the delight of rail enthusiasts—and to the dismay of passengers who saw their rattan seats, gloomy interiors, and faltering ceiling fans as anything but charming. Even after they were re-equipped with new-generation electric m.u. cars, the electrified services shared Lackawanna Terminal's platforms with a smaller number of diesel-powered trains, all of which were operated by newly formed New Jersey Transit—also the terminal's new owner—after 1979. At that time, a respectable 239 weekday trains (136 electrified and 97 diesel-powered) met the needs of approximately 60,000 daily passengers.

As the twentieth century ended, Lackawanna Terminal found itself the beneficiary of a comprehensive rehabilitation, befitting its status as NJ Transit's "crown jewel." Ferry service had returned in a modest way, operated by NY Waterways to Manhattan's World Financial Center, and a light-rail facility was under construction adjacent to the venerable "heavy rail" terminal. NJ Transit restored the 1907 structure's interior to pristine condition.

NEW PENNSYLVANIA R. R. STATION, NEWARK, N. J. 16

5A-H841

The Pennsylvania Railroad's Newark terminal was designed by McKim, Mead & White a quarter century after they created Manhattan's Pennsylvania Station, and exhibits traces of Beaux-Arts influence amid the Modern Classicism in favor during the 1930s.—JOE WELSH COLLECTION

Another terminal in the shadow of Manhattan is another Pennsylvania Station, that in downtown Newark, New Jersey, that state's largest city. Built by the City of Newark and the mighty Pennsylvania Railroad, the Art Deco gem opened in 1935. The depot building for the $42 million station project was designed by McKim, Mead & White—the same architectural team that designed New York's Pennsylvania Station. It was a true intermodal center, its four levels serving PRR intercity and suburban trains entering or leaving New York City on the New York–Philadelphia main line, Lehigh Valley trains (which used the PRR to reach Manhattan), rapid-transit trains of the Hudson & Manhattan (today's PATH system) "tubes," vehicular traffic, and a myriad of Newark city bus, subway, and trolley routes. After a major restructuring of northeastern Jersey suburban train services in 1966, Reading and Jersey Central trains began originating and terminating at Newark Penn Station.

The restored post-classical depot today features waiting-room benches emblazoned with Pennsylvania Railroad keystone logos and globed chandeliers in a waiting room/ticketing lobby that exudes all the symmetry and stateliness expected of a big city terminal. The multi through-track (on a sweeping curve, no less) design with high-level platforms efficiently handles numerous Amtrak, New Jersey Transit and PATH trains and thousands of arriving and departing passengers, including numerous patrons who must change trains (or modes) at Newark.

With its sweeping, curved facade partially obscured by the Atlantic Avenue elevated railway and a broad awning along Summer Street, Boston's South Station is shown as it appeared very early in the twentieth century. The structure, designed by the firm of Shepley, Rutan & Coolidge, hosted its first revenue train on January 1, 1899. A granite eagle surveyed Dewey Square from its perch atop the terminal's 12-foot clock.
—KEVIN HOLLAND COLLECTION

Continued from page 25
River shore on the revamped ex-NYC West Side Freight Line to a new connection leading into Penn Station.

On May 25, 1999, the U.S. federal government, Amtrak, the U.S. Postal Service, and associated New York state agencies announced ambitious plans to create a "new" Penn Station within McKim, Mead & White's Beaux-Arts U.S. Post Office building immediately west of the post-1963 Madison Square Garden/Penn Station complex. The colonnaded postal structure was built over the PRR's electrified tracks to facilitate handling of the huge volume of mail once carried and sorted aboard the railroad's trains. Spurred by Senator Daniel Patrick Moynihan, the three-year project was intended, in the words of then-U.S. President Clinton, to "honor one of the first great buildings of the twentieth century, and create the first great public building of the twenty-first century." Plans for the new $315 million Penn Station combined a physical restoration and adaptive reuse of the postal building with a new soaring glassed atrium that will serve as Amtrak's ticketing area. The new train concourse area also benefits from the natural light provided by a renewed skylight canopy—not unlike the famous glass-roof concourse of the original Pennsylvania Station.

BOSTON

The notion of Boston as a cultural buffer between "Northeast" and "Down East" was made all the more tangible by the separation between—and the naming of—the city's two main railroad terminals. If the urban and urbane Northeast ended at South Station's bumper posts, then New England most assuredly began across town at North Station. This had more to do with the personalities of the railroads and the trains serving the two depots than with the stations themselves.

South Station

Of the two terminals, South Station was, and is, the decidedly more impressive, even in its latter-day truncated form. South Station served passengers of the New York, New Haven & Hartford Railroad and its subsidiaries along with the Boston & Albany Railroad, and early in its existence held the title of America's busiest railroad terminal to the tune of over 700 trains each day moving as many as 40 million passengers annually. The B&A ultimately fell under New York Central's far-flung web of influence and offered passenger schedules between South Station, Springfield, Pittsfield, Albany, and points west over the NYC.

The New Haven, on the other hand, was a cosmopolitan artery to New York's Pennsylvania Station (and beyond, via PRR connections and through cars), along with well-equipped secondary and branchline trains to points as diverse as Cape Cod and Pittsfield, Mass.

South Station owes its creation to the fragmented nature of Boston's railroad network in the late nineteenth century and to a resultant desire on the part of politicians and passengers alike to reduce the number of terminals from the eight then in service. The first big step in this direction was taken in 1894 when the Boston & Maine Railroad and three affiliated companies consolidated their four separate terminals into the first North Station. With the precedent having been established across town, Boston Mayor J. P. Quincy urged the New Haven and B&A in 1896 to collaborate toward a similar objective. The result was the creation that same year of the Boston Terminal Company (BTC), majority control of which (80 percent) rested with the New Haven and its subsidiaries.

Ground was broken in January 1897 and by the end of that year the plans of the architectural firm of Shepley, Rutan & Coolidge began to take shape in steel, brick, and Connecticut granite. The site chosen, fronting Summer Street between Dorchester Avenue and Atlantic Avenue, had been the location of one of the four depots that South Station would replace. Enlarged to 35 acres to accommodate the new terminal, the BTC's property abutted Fort Point Channel, the tidal waters of which had to be restrained by a coffer-

The headlight of an arriving Amtrak train highlighted South Station's complex trackwork and antiquated semaphore signals in January 1982.—MIKE SCHAFER

South Station's two owners were represented on July 2, 1967, by an outbound New Haven train behind a pair of FL9s, and New York Central S-2 No. 9656 switching head-end cars. The large REA sign marks the terminal's express wing along Atlantic Avenue.—KEVIN HOLLAND COLLECTION

dam and seawall lest potential flooding disrupt operation of the new terminal.

The Shepley, Rutan & Coolidge plan treated the property as an open-ended rectangle, three sides of which were formed by the 2,189-foot long combination of five-story head house and two-story baggage-handling structures. The headhouse design lent a rounded corner to the rectangle where it faced what became Dewey Square. The long flanks of the site were occupied by the terminal's baggage and express facilities, with outbound business handled on the Atlantic Avenue (west) side, and inbound head-end traffic accommodated on the Dorchester Avenue wing, along with the terminal's power house. Within the generous confines of the rectangle, the architects incorporated 28 platform tracks which they covered with an immense

In stark contrast to the years of South Station's nadir, the waiting room/concourse atrium area today is alive with intercity passengers, commuters, and vendors. The atrium area, shown in this 1998 scene that looks in from one of the train gates, replaced the original Midway; the depot head house stands at right in background.—MIKE SCHAFER

650 x 710-foot balloon train shed. The open south end of the rectangle contained the station's particularly complex throat and approach trackage, overseen by a 165-lever interlocking plant controlling 238 track switches and nine semaphore signal bridges.

Despite its huge size and capacity, the terminal's designers and owners were concerned that it would not adequately accommodate projected commuter traffic. After discarding as impractical a scheme for two-level trackage in the platform area, they settled on a pair of underground loop tracks and associated platform space to be electrified and devoted exclusively to commuter trains running on

headways as close as two minutes. Although the loop facilities were indeed built, they were never electrified and thus were never used for their intended purpose; the exhaust smoke of steam locomotives made their operation through the loop impractical. The tunnels eventually were severed, and the clatter of bowling pins later echoed through the lower level.

Boston's South Station was formally dedicated on December 28, 1898, and the first New Haven revenue trains were handled on New Year's Day 1899. The first B&A movements occurred on July 23, 1899, and trains over what would become the New Haven's main line to its namesake Connecticut community and New York City followed on September 10. By the end of its first year, South Station was handling almost 750 trains each day—of which only a third were intercity schedules.

Within the original head house, a restaurant, women's waiting room, and 65 x 225-foot main waiting room were provided for intercity passengers, while the 600 x 100-foot "Midway" concourse area gave commuters direct street access through the station's columned main entrance on Dewey Square. The Midway was essentially an extension of the train shed until 1930, when it was closed in as part of the huge balloon structure's removal and replacement with umbrella-type platform canopies. As with so many of its counterparts, the terminal was pressed to its limits by World War II. Approximately 46 million passengers passed through in 1945 alone.

South Station also shared the postwar fate of the passenger trains it served, and just two decades after the war witnessed passenger levels barely one-tenth of 1945's traffic peak. Intercity and commuter trains alike were discontinued at an accelerating pace, to the point that fewer than 100 daily trains were being handled when South Station changed hands in 1965, four years after the New Haven and its BTC subsidiary entered bankruptcy. The Boston Redevelopment Authority (BRA) paid just under $7 million for the terminal, which had seen the eastern half of its platform trackage replaced by a postal facility. The new owner intended to raze the facility to make way for an office development, and demolition did indeed begin in 1972. At the eleventh hour, after both baggage wings and the eastern portion of the head house had been destroyed, further demolition was suspended as the BRA began to look upon the redevelopment from a more sensitive perspective. The curved portion of the head house—with its columned facade, 14-foot clock, and 8-foot stone eagle—was saved to become South Station's latter-day incarnation.

Inside the station, new intercity operator Amtrak reopened the long-closed (and partially demolished) main waiting room. July 1978 saw the station sold again, this time to Boston's commuter agency, the Massachusetts Bay Transportation Authority. The MBTA, responsible for the

city's commuter rail service, contracted first with Conrail and, after March 1977, with south-side interloper Boston & Maine to operate the terminal's remaining suburban services. (Conrail was the 1976 successor to Penn Central, which itself was the product of the 1968 merger of the New York Central and Pennsylvania railroads and in turn merged with the New Haven in 1969.)

Between 1984 and 1990, $195 million was spent to thoroughly refurbish South Station as a multimodal transportation center. The relocation of passengers to a temporary station from 1984 to 1988 permitted a complete renovation of the surviving head house, during which a sec-

tion of the long-gone Atlantic Avenue portion was even replicated—right down to granite quarried from the original 1897 source. Track and signaling improvements were made—at the expense of the station's trademark semaphore blades—and a total of 11 high-level platforms were built to allow easier and faster loading and unloading of trains. A three-story atrium evoked the airiness of the station's original Midway, while Amtrak's Boston Division and other tenants moved into the station's refurbished office space. These developments were but a prelude to the late-1990s extension of electrified Amtrak Northeast Corridor service beyond New Haven to Boston, which saw South Station

Until 1930, South Station's platform tracks were protected from the elements by this massive 650 x 710-foot train shed. This October 19, 1929, view gives the "lay of the land," from the Dorchester Avenue bridge across Fort Point Channel in the foreground to the Atlantic Avenue express wing. The depressed tracks at right led to the innovative underground commuter loops that were never used for their intended purpose.—PETER CARROLL, BOB STANLEY COLLECTION

finally linked under wire to its corridor counterparts in New York (Penn Station), Philadelphia, and Washington.

North Station

Across town, Boston's first North Station (opened in 1894) was an imposing building that met the needs of the B&M well into the 1920s. Its replacement, located deep in the bowels of the 1928 Boston Garden sports arena, was decidedly less apparent from the street. The structure was known from its November 1928 opening as the home of the Boston Bruins hockey team and, after 1946, of basketball's Boston Celtics. For many years a large neon rooftop sign confirmed to unsure travelers that this was, indeed, also the site of the B&M's North Station. The mass of the Art Deco structure's rather spartan Causeway Street facade was lessened by seven groups of vertical windows. Next door, the high-rise Hotel Manger was actually an integral part of the station/arena complex.

Any anonymity on the part of North Station vanished, though, when the terminal was viewed from trackside.

With the sterile facade of the arena's north wall as a backdrop, 23 stub platform tracks abruptly funneled into four double-track throats which crossed the Charles River on a like number of massive rolling lift bridges. So close was the station to the river, in fact, that much of the throat trackage was supported by pilings over the water.

Station tracks were arranged so that trains destined for Portland, Maine, and intermediate points arrived and departed from the eastern half of the complex, while trains using the B&M's New Hampshire and Fitchburg main lines to destinations including Troy, New York, White River Junction, and Montreal used the western half.

The clouds of smoke from a catastrophic six-alarm bridge fire on January 20, 1984, held an unlikely silver lining in the form of the opportunity, while rail access to the station was already severed, to rebuild the terminal's trackage and platforms. In the 15-month interim, passengers were accommodated across the Charles River at a temporary station at the B&M's East Cambridge yard and made their way downtown aboard shuttle buses. When North

This late afternoon panorama captured North Station on a typical day in June 1952. A quartet of Boston & Maine commuter trains awaits their passengers at left, while the Portland-bound streamliner *Pine Tree* stands at center behind a B&M Electro-Motive E7A. One of three Canadian Pacific E8 locomotives purchased for joint Montreal–Boston service marks the overnight *Red Wing*, while the *Cheshire* at far right awaits its departure to White River Junction, Vermont. The latter train's equipment was delivered in 1935 as the jointly operated Boston & Maine-Maine Central *Flying Yankee*, a Budd-built stainless-steel streamliner that put North Station on the map as a vanguard in lightweight-train operation. Over the years, the little streamliner—nicknamed the "Silver Slipper"—operated under a variety of different train names, but was a regular in B&M's Boston terminal.—JIM SHAUGHNESSY

Boston's North Station is idealized in this colorized postcard from circa 1930. Integral to the station complex was the Hotel Manger, at left, which was connected directly to the terminal. Compare this view with the photo below.—MIKE SCHAFER COLLECTION

The facade of North Station was actually quite hemmed-in by other structures, including one of Boston's elevated railway lines, as illustrated in this view from August 1952.—JOHN DZIOBKO

Station reopened on April 20, 1985, a total of $12 million had been spent to repair the burned bridge and upgrade the station's tracks, platforms, and signaling.

Long-sought plans to replace Boston Garden finally came to fruition in 1995 with the opening of the $160-million Fleet Center immediately north of the old structure. The railroad terminal's decade-old refurbished platforms and trackage were retained, served by a new station facility once again located deep within the sports and entertainment complex. The Fleet Center officially opened on October 7, 1995, just over a week after a final National Hockey League exhibition game had been played to close out the Garden's career. Two years later, on October 31, 1997, the task of demolishing the former station/arena structure began. This was a painstaking process, since the Fleet Center was, in some spots, barely 12 inches from the old building. Complicating matters further, debris had to be hauled away at night to avoid disrupting the area's already congested traffic.

In its post-1995 incarnation, the MBTA's North Station became a 12-track facility—the number of active tracks was temporarily reduced, however, to accommodate road construction related to Boston's "Big Dig." The new station's waiting room doubles as the Fleet Center's main crowd entrance, which quickly proved to be an untenable mix when event schedules conflicted with peak commuter periods.

After an absence of almost four decades, intercity rail passenger service will return to North Station when Amtrak's long-delayed trains to Portland, Maine, make their debut. Since early proposals to incorporate an Amtrak rail link between Boston's two terminals as part of the Big Dig expressway project could secure neither funding nor political support, Amtrak service from North Station will remain disconnected from the rest of the Northeast Corridor.

NORTHERN NEW ENGLAND

Portland Union Station

Portland Union Station served as the point of connection between the Maine Central (MEC) and Boston & Maine railroads and their jointly operated passenger trains between Boston's North Station and Bangor, Maine. Seven of the station's nine through tracks were devoted to passenger trains, with the remaining pair handling freight traffic as part of the Maine Central's main line from nearby Rigby Yard. The lanky Romanesque terminal, accented by an assortment of turrets and a clock tower, was noted for its fireplace-equipped waiting room.

Portland Union Station was a "multimodal" terminal before the term came into vogue. This was attributable to its owners' enlightened integration of pre-World War II bus, airline, and passenger train operations. On the station's latter-day marquee sign, "Portland Union Station" and "Portland Bus Terminal" had virtually equal billing.

In its heyday, the station handled through cars to points as distant as New York and Washington, D.C., and was an early haunt of one the first lightweight streamlined trains in the country, the Budd-built stainless steel *Flying Yankee* of 1935. In its earliest years of joint B&M-MEC operation, this articulated trainset operated between Boston, Portland, and Bangor. With its location between the population centers of the Northeast and the resort areas of northern New England, the station also handled seasonal moves ranging from youngsters' camp trains to the all-Pullman *Bar Harbor Express*.

September 6, 1960, was the final day of passenger train operation at Portland Union Station. After the arrival of B&M train 1 from Boston, the station was closed. The station's final departure occurred the day before, as MEC train 9 left on its last eastbound run for Vanceboro, Maine.

The station was demolished less than a year later to make way for a strip mall and parking lot. On August 31, 1961, the stone clock tower, seemingly built for the ages, came crashing to the ground to join the pile of granite rubble that had been Portland Union Station.

Bangor Union Station

Bangor Union Station, built in 1907 as a through station, was as far beyond Portland as most Maine Central passengers traveled. In the postwar era, only the *Gull* continued beyond Bangor in each direction on the MEC, and at that only until the international pool run to Canada's Maritime provinces was discontinued in 1960.

The compact brownstone and buff brick Tuscan-influenced structure measured 82 x 154 feet and featured a 130-foot-tall clock tower. A 22-foot-wide *porte-cochere*

sheltered the building's main entrance, through which the 41 x 84-foot marble-floored general waiting room was reached. A smoking room, ladies waiting room, newsstand, ticket office, and baggage room were located off the main waiting room. A 41 x 60-foot dining room occupied the remainder of the ground floor, with offices above. Behind the station, a 500 x 100-foot train shed sheltered passengers and crews alike and was of at least some benefit during the winter.

Bangor Union Station also served the Bangor & Aroostook (BAR) Railroad's modest schedules to the far reaches of northern Maine. These connections once included through coaches and sleeping cars to Boston's North Station via the Maine Central and B&M. As the BAR moved to discontinue its passenger trains in favor of buses in the

continued on page 38

Portland Union Station was the gateway to a northwoods vacation for generations of camp-bound summer travelers. Sadly, the Romanesque terminal was demolished in August 1961, almost exactly a year after the Maine Central discontinued its portion of Boston–Bangor through services operated jointly with the Boston & Maine.—KEVIN HOLLAND COLLECTION

Bangor Union Station marked the northern end of what in today's context would have been considered a "corridor" from Boston. This was Maine Central and Bangor & Aroostook country, as demonstrated by the truss-rod-equipped and stainless-steel-sheathed coaches at right, but the B&M E-unit was equally at home thanks to schedules operated in conjunction with the Maine Central.—BOB'S PHOTOS, KEVIN HOLLAND COLLECTION

HINTERLAND NEW ENGLAND TERMINALS

In a scene to warm a Budd Company salesperson's heart, White River Junction's Colonial Revival station is a hub of late-1950s Boston & Maine activity as Budd Rail Diesel Car trains (left to right, from Boston, Massachusetts; Springfield, Massachusetts; and Berlin, New Hampshire) exchange passengers. This view faces southeast, with Central Vermont tracks (over which the B&M had running rights) to the right.—KEVIN T. FARRELL COLLECTION

Nestled at the confluence of the Connecticut and White rivers in rural central Vermont, the Colonial Revival brick station at White River Junction seems, at a glance, out of place. When considered against the backdrop of pre-Interstate traffic generated by Dartmouth College, the nearby Ivy League school, however, the distinctive station's size and style makes a great deal more sense.

Opened on December 8, 1937, to replace outmoded earlier facilities that had been destroyed by fire, the 50 x 100-foot brick structure hosted over 30 daily trains in its prime. While many of these were through trains merely making station stops, enough trains originated and terminated at White River Junction—or had cars added and removed for such endpoints as New York, Boston, and Washington—to qualify the spot as a bonafide terminal. Although not officially referred to as such, it was also very much

a "union" station, owned by the Central Vermont and Boston & Maine railroads. By virtue of its owners' international through-train partnerships, cars and locomotives from the Canadian Pacific Railway and rolling stock lettered for the New Haven Railroad and Canadian National Railway were also regular visitors to the station.

Although modest in size, the station nonetheless offered passengers a 51 x 25-foot waiting room—with Colonial chairs instead of the usual benches—and a small restaurant. Baggage and express business was accommodated in an annex on the station's north side, and a small wooden platform canopy provided outdoor shelter on the south side. Prominent signage directed passengers to the appropriate platforms, as CV-B&M through services were assigned to the west side of the structure and CPR-B&M trains to the east. Since the CV main line ran between the station and town center, a pedestrian subway was provided from the station platform.

Following years of declining traffic and selective train discontinuances, the station's owners ceased all passenger service to White River Junction in September 1966. Amtrak restored the former Montrealer/Washingtonian in October 1972 and has served the station in various guises ever since, despite occasional brief hiatuses and the discontinuance of international operation over this route north of St. Albans, Vermont. As of 2001, Amtrak's Vermonter serves White River Junction and St. Albans, Vermont.

Northern New England had no shortage of hinterland terminals like White River Junction. Similarly grand structures, seemingly at odds with their rural surroundings, could be found in places like St. Albans and North Conway, New Hampshire. Just 117 miles north of White River Junction on the CV main line and serving many of the same trains, St. Albans was especially noted for its brick-facade balloon train shed adjoining the CV's

1867 headquarters building. Until the deteriorating trainshed was demolished in September 1963, the sight of diesel-powered streamlined trains emerging from its four arched portals was an everyday anachronism.

North Conway's marvelous twin-turreted wood-frame station, built in 1874 and remembered by generations of weekend skiers as the terminus of the Boston & Maine's "Snow Train" excursions from Boston, survives as the restored centerpiece of the Conway Scenic Railroad. North Conway was typical—in function if not in architecture—of similar "resort terminals" throughout North America, at places like French Lick, Indiana; White Sulphur Springs, West Virginia.; Grand Canyon, Arizona; and Banff, Alberta. Railroading's "golden age" saw special trains and private cars destined to these unlikely outposts, in order for the cars' occupants to enjoy the benefits of their destinations before the automobile and the airplane achieved supremacy. In common with their large urban counterparts, these vest-pocket terminals had to maintain switching, storage, and servicing facilities to support their largely seasonal traffic.

With little room to spare, Canadian National U-1 Northern No. 6173 pokes through St. Albans' 1867 train shed with CV train 20, the *Washingtonian*, on March 28, 1956. The ornate timber-framed shed, with brick facades at its north and south ends, was razed in 1963.—JIM SHAUGHNESSY

Exuding every bit as much solidity as the railroad that built it, the PRR's Thirtieth Street Station overlooks the Schuylkill River. The bridge in the background of this June 1986 view carries suburban-service tracks from downtown Philadelphia to the station's upper level. Mainline trains run through the lower level, parallel to the river. PRR "limiteds" operating between New York, Pittsburgh, and other points west did not serve Thirtieth Street, calling instead at North Philadelphia station to avoid a reverse move.—MIKE SCHAFER

The west portico's classical columns—seen here on March 18, 2000—were an unusual touch in a station whose interior featured understated Art Deco elegance.—JOE GREENSTEIN

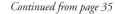

Continued from page 35
late 1950s, the road's trains vacated Bangor Union Station and instead originated and terminated at the BAR's offices in Northern Maine Junction, several miles west of Bangor on the Maine Central main line to Portland.

When solitary occupant Maine Central discontinued its remaining passenger trains effective September 6, 1960, Bangor Union Station was closed. MEC continued to operate dedicated mail-and-express trains on passenger train schedules for a few years, but these trains were serviced in Bangor at the railroad's freight yard. The railroad sold the station property to developers, and Bangor Union Station was demolished in November 1961.

PHILADELPHIA

Philadelphia was hardly a one-railroad town, although the Pennsylvania Railroad had a knack for sometimes making it seem that way to outsiders, leaving Monopoly-board rivals Baltimore & Ohio and hometown Reading Railroad very much in its Tuscan red shadow.

The Pennsy had its headquarters in the city, and it was in Philadelphia that the railroad's New York–Washington racetrack was intersected by the "Broad Way" Main Line (yes, on the PRR, this line was a proper noun) that reached west to Harrisburg and across the Alleghenies to Pittsburgh and points beyond.

Thirtieth Street Station and its close relatives

Thirtieth Street was a comparatively late instance in North America of a new terminal being created, in part, as a result of civic urging to reduce downtown congestion. The product of the Chicago architectural partnership of Graham, Anderson, Probst & White, Thirtieth Street Station was originally named Pennsylvania Station and—in conjunction with its downtown contemporary, Suburban Station—replaced a pair of obsolescent PRR terminals, Broad Street and West Philadelphia stations.

Broad Street Station dated from December 1881 and was a stub-ended downtown facility at Market and 15th streets whose tracks approached on what came to be known locally as the "Chinese Wall," a right-of-way embankment that effectively split Philadelphia's core for a distance of roughly a half-mile.

West Philadelphia was a companion station located on Market Street, two blocks west of where the new Thirtieth Street Station would be built between 1929 and 1933 adjacent to the Schuylkill (SKOO-kul) River. The new Thirtieth Street Station was designed to accommodate both intercity and commuter traffic with an innovative and effective two-level plan. A new electrified, eight-track downtown terminal, Suburban Station, opened in 1930 with subway trackage replacing the Chinese Wall. Despite its operational replacement, much of the embankment—along with Broad Street Station itself—would endure until the early 1950s, its removal protracted by the Depression and World War II. When it was finally gone, the 18 or so acres of prime city-center railroad-owned real estate became the Penn Center complex. From the street, Suburban Station took the form of a 22-story Art Deco office tower, known today as One Penn Center at Suburban Station.

Operationally, trains based at Suburban Station traveled to and from the city's suburbs by way of Thirtieth

Broad Street Station, which also housed the PRR's headquarters, opened in 1881 and served Pennsylvania Railroad passengers in conjunction with West Philadelphia station.—MIKE SCHAFER COLLECTION

Philadelphia's other, non-Pennsylvania Railroad terminals included the Baltimore & Ohio's modest facility at 24th and Chestnut Streets, known simply (as the sign indicates) as "B&O Station." Philadelphia was essentially the easternmost point on the B&O; east of the city, B&O trains were relayed to Jersey City via the Reading and Jersey Central railroads.—ED BIRCH COLLECTION

Reading Company had its own terminal in the heart of downtown Philadelphia. The stub-end facility mainly served suburban runs, such as this electric multiple-unit (m.u.) train departing in 1966. Trains no longer call at Reading Terminal, which today is an upscale marketplace.—MIKE MC BRIDE

Street Station's six-track upper level. In the 1980s, under the auspices of the Southeastern Pennsylvania Transportation Authority (SEPTA), Suburban Station became a through facility when an underground connection was made with former Reading Railroad commuter routes via the Market East station.

Thirtieth Street itself opened in two stages. The upper-level commuter station was first, serving its initial passengers on September 28, 1930, the same day that Suburban Station opened its doors. Intercity passengers made their first use of Thirtieth Street's still-incomplete lower level on March 12, 1933. The 327 x 637-foot terminal was built over the through tracks, a layout made possible by the Pennsy's mainline and suburban electrification which eliminated the problems of smoke permeating the station from below. The upper-level suburban tracks are perpendicular to the intercity trackage below and reach the station from downtown on an integral bridge across the Schuylkill River. The terminal's rather severe exterior and interior design reflect the Modern Classicism seen in many public buildings of the time in North America and Europe as the Art Deco movement evolved. The terminal's marble-floored concourse measures 135 x 290 feet x 95 feet high, with Art Deco ornamentation complementing an imposing coffered ceiling.

Its location astride the Northeast Corridor spared Thirtieth Street from the depths of decline experienced by so many of North America's great terminals, although long-distance services to Florida suffered before and after the Pennsy became part of ill-fated Penn Central in 1968. Amtrak moved in in 1971, and SEPTA assumed responsibility for the city's commuter rail services, including those serving Thirtieth Street and Suburban stations.

During the 1990s, Amtrak invested over $11 million to renovate Thirtieth Street Station, ensuring a bright future for this classic terminal.

WASHINGTON UNION STATION

This pearl in the nation's capital is, above all, a survivor. From a wayward locomotive crashing through its floors to political fiascos that very nearly destroyed it, Washington Union Station has weathered pitfalls to emerge as a remarkably restored, vibrant facility, still—in contrast to many of its ilk—fulfilling its original purpose.

The concept of a union station for Washington developed in the earliest years of the twentieth century. In 1901, a newly passed federal law required the owners of the city's two existing steam railroad terminals to vacate their locations in a push to eliminate the hazards and inconvenience of multiple grade crossings. The Pennsylvania Railroad station—occupying the site of today's National Gallery of Art—and the Baltimore & Ohio station at C Street N.W. and New Jersey Avenue were ordered replaced, but with

LEFT: The creation of Washington Union Station was a high point of the "City Beautiful" movement, an urban design esthetic that gained momentum after the World's Columbian Exposition of 1893 in Chicago. Architect Daniel H. Burnham's Beaux-Arts vision takes shape in this circa-1906 construction view of the capital's new terminal. Stonework on the main entrance is well underway as steelwork continues.—KEVIN HOLLAND COLLECTION

BELOW: Washington Union Station is shown in the 1940s when travelers could still take a streetcar to the station. A patina of grime on the building's exterior reflects Union Station's four-plus decades of service to the nation's capital. —KEVIN HOLLAND COLLECTION

Washington Union Station's Great Hall under construction circa 1908.
—KEVIN HOLLAND COLLECTION

The Great Hall, completed and serving in its original capacity as a waiting room.
—MIKE SCHAFER COLLECTION

Newly renovated, the Great Hall today is multi-functional, serving as a concourse, information area, and restaurant and banquet seating.—MIKE SCHAFER

two independent facilities. Concurrently, the Senate's McMillan Commission was establishing guidelines intended to render downtown Washington more faithful to the 1789 plans of Pierre L'Enfant, in which parks, boulevards, and monumental public architecture figured prominently. By the time the Commission issued its report in January 1902, the requirement for a pair of competing rail terminals had been dropped in favor of a grand union station to be located in the shadow of the Capitol at Delaware and Massachusetts Avenues. When President Theodore Roosevelt authorized construction of a "union station in the District of Columbia" in February 1903, Washington Union Station was born.

With ties to both the McMillan Commission and the PRR, Chicago architect, city planner, and "City Beautiful" advocate Daniel H. Burnham (1846–1912) won the commission to design Washington's new station. Ground was broken on April 15, 1905, for a $16-million project encompassing the station itself, trackwork and approaches, a coach yard, car shop, and engine terminal. Reflecting the pre-eminence of passenger trains in early twentieth century America, the facilities were designed with enough excess capacity to accommodate the quadrennial crush of traffic created by presidential inaugurations.

The white marble and granite head house measures 211 x 663 feet, enclosing a general waiting room of 220 x 130 feet x 93 feet high. As built, the station's concourse measured 170 x 760 feet and was billed as the largest room in the world at the time of its construction. The PRR made a similar claim for the waiting room of New York's Pennsylvania

An aerial view of Washington Union Station from the 1950s shows the head house, platform trackage, and throat to good advantage. Through tracks serving the Capitol Hill tunnel are at left. The trapezoidal structure next to the station is the main Post Office; to its right is the U.S. Government Printing Office, served by a spur from the station. The rectangular structure at bottom center is the Railway Express Agency building.—KEVIN HOLLAND COLLECTION

Station in 1910, apparently using a different definition of "largest" or "room" since the latter space was measurably smaller at 277 x 103 x 150 feet high.

A total of 33 platform tracks were provided in Washington's new station, with the platforms themselves up to 900 feet long. Thirteen through tracks carried trains to and from the Potomac River and points south via a double-track tunnel under Capitol Hill, while 20 stub-end tracks handled traffic originating and terminating at the station.

The station opened for traffic on October 27, 1907, with the arrival of B&O train No. 10 from Pittsburgh. The first PRR trains did not arrive until November 17, 1907. The complex operated under the auspices of the Washington Terminal Company (WT), originally a B&O subsidiary and a legacy of the 1901 station relocation order. By the time Union Station opened, the WT facilities were jointly owned by the PRR and B&O. Other railroads contracted for terminal and station services as tenants. All switching was handled by a fleet of WT-lettered locomotives in both the steam and diesel eras.

Union Station's tracks were electrified on January 28, 1935, as the culmination of the PRR's massive electrification of its New York-Washington main line. The debut of the Pennsy's sleek and powerful GG1 electric motors cut the railroad's previous best travel time over the route by 40 minutes, to just over 3 1/2 hours. One of these GG1s made headlines in 1953 when, failing to stop with the inbound

Federal in tow, it crashed past its assigned end-of-track bumper on the station's stub-ended track 16, entered the station concourse, and fell through the floor into the basement. Remarkably, not a soul was injured—and the redoubtable GG1 was extricated and returned to service shortly thereafter.

At the height of the postwar period, the intercity trains of seven railroads called on WUS. In addition to landlords B&O and PRR, tenant roads included Richmond, Fredericksburg & Potomac; Atlantic Coast Line; Seaboard Air Line; Southern; and Chesapeake & Ohio. Attrition through the merger movement of the 1960s saw C&O gain control of B&O, while ACL and SAL combined to form Seaboard Coast Line in 1967. The PRR disappeared into Penn Central in 1968.

The tracks of Washington Union Station afforded an outstanding—and colorful—window on the contrasts of postwar American railroading. The ever-staid Pennsy rubbed its electrified shoulders here with Southern connections ranging from the genteel to the downright gregarious. In the days before reliable and widely affordable airline service, the volume of passenger traffic between New York, Florida, and intermediate points sustained some of the most colorful and competitive passenger trains in the country, and they all passed through Washington Union Station. Perhaps the most colorful was the *Orange Blossom Special*, a seasonal Seaboard Air Line train whose externally unremarkable green Pullmans were pulled by streamlined General Motors E4 locomotives decked out in a stunning "citrus" paint scheme of yellow, orange, and green. This was a train whose destination could only be Florida, as were the later purple-and-stainless steel streamliners of rival Atlantic Coast Line. Trains of both SAL and ACL reached Washington over the rails of the RF&P from Richmond, crossing the Potomac at Alexandria, Virginia, and traversing the short tunnel under Capitol Hill before emerging on the station's through tracks.

While urban terminals across the country were lucky to host any trains after Amtrak took over the nation's greatly diminished passenger train network on May 1, 1971, Washington Union Station could still claim two non-Amtrak intercity tenants. The Southern Railway declined to join Amtrak until February 1, 1979, and in the intervening period of nearly eight years operated its overnight *Southern Crescent* between Washington and New Orleans.

Those same eight years marked a period of profound change for the station, stemming from 1968 federal legislation paving the way to convert the structure into a National Visitor Center in time for the Bicentennial celebrations of 1976. The project, which cost over $120 million, accomplished little beyond creating a gaping 8,000-square foot pit in the station's Main Hall for an intended audio-visual orientation program, and relegating

Where passengers once scrambled to and from trains or waited in groups at gates to board, passengers and pedestrians today browse and buy. Washington Union Station's concourse area has perhaps changed the most radically. What was originally, for the public, a single-level area is today three levels featuring numerous shops and—in what was the baggage-marshalling area in the basement—a food court. This is the area where, in 1953, the *Federal* from Boston was the victim of an unusual brake failure that caused the train to crash through the bumping post and into the concourse area as horrified passengers ran for safety. The weight of the train's GG1 electric locomotive caused the floor to collapse, and the locomotive tumbled into the basement level where people today munch bagels.—ALEX MAYES

Amtrak passengers to a cramped and hard-to-find replacement station. A steady stream of inquiries at the National Park Service's Visitor Center came from bewildered Amtrak passengers looking for the "new" station.

The ignominious Visitor Center lasted barely two years, and by early 1981 the station was in such a state of structural decay that it was closed completely. The building's heating, plumbing, and other essential systems had not benefited from the Visitor Center funds. The roof leaked, and chunks of the ceiling were beginning to fall away. Recognizing that steps had to be taken to solve the station's problems, the Union Station Redevelopment Act was passed by Congress later in 1981. Embraced by then-Transportation Secretary Elizabeth Dole, this legislation marked the turning point in Union Station's fortunes. In the ensuing seven years, under the auspices of the Union Station Redevelopment Corporation, the structure was stabilized, and between 1986 and 1988 it was restored both as an architectural treasure and a fully functional railroad terminal.

Washington Union Station reopened with great fanfare on September 29, 1988. On November 1, 1988, title passed to the U.S. Department of Transportation, which purchased the facility from the heirs of its railroad owners and leased space to Amtrak and a range of retail and commercial tenants. At the time of its reopening, WUS was ranked as Amtrak's third-busiest station, after New York's Penn Station and Thirtieth Street in Philadelphia.

Today, WUS remains the southern anchor of Amtrak's Northeast Corridor, the 457-mile high-speed electrified rail line linking the nation's capital with Baltimore, Philadelphia, New York, and Boston. Reflecting the District of Columbia's historic and geographic ties, Union Station was, and is, also a point of connection between the high-density services of the Northeast and long-distance trains to and from Florida and the Southeast, as well as Chicago.

THROUGH THE HEARTLAND ③

•CINCINNATI •CLEVELAND • DETROIT • MILWAUKEE • ST. LOUIS

ABOVE: The entrance to the old Terminal Hotel portion of St. Louis Union Station has acquired a revitalized look since the entire station complex was revamped and redeveloped in the 1980s.
—MIKE SCHAFER

FACING PAGE: This is the Chicago & North Western's lakefront depot in Milwaukee, Wisconsin, looking northward on a late afternoon in February 1962. The Electro-Motive E-series locomotive is waiting in the sidelines to take train 160, the *Streamliner "400"*, to Chicago.
—JIM BOYD

America's heartland—that expansive region loosely defined by the Ohio River on the east, the U.S.-Canadian border on the north, the western ends of Nebraska, Kansas, Oklahoma and the Dakotas, and the Mason-Dixon line on the south—was home to a wide array of railroads. Many heartland cities served as gateways between carriers based in the East, West, and South as well as step-off points for numerous railroads integral to the heartland itself. Small wonder, then, that the heart of America was rife with railroad terminals, particularly "union"-type stations. In fact, to the Midwest goes the distinction of the first union station in the U.S., opened at Indianapolis in September 1853.

Variety made heartland terminals particularly fascinating—not only in terms of architecture and design, but in the railroads that served them. Here one could witness great limiteds from the East Coast mingling with the likes of the *Super Chief, City of Portland*, or the *California Zephyr*; or watch as Southern's *New Royal Palm* from Florida glided into Cincinnati to deliver connecting passengers to trains dispersing them to Chicago, Detroit, Cleveland, and St. Louis.

CINCINNATI UNION TERMINAL

Fellheimer & Wagner merged elements of Art Deco and Modern Classicism in their Cincinnati Union Terminal. After falling on hard times with the demise of the trains and railroads it served, CUT's head house—shown here in August 1999—was splendidly restored as a museum center. Following an absence of almost 19 years, Amtrak even returned to the terminal in 1991.
—MIKE SCHAFER

In the early years of the twentieth century, Ohio's "Queen City" was served by a total of seven trunk-line railroads operating five separate passenger stations. This diverse group of old, scattered facilities had a common bond, though—the frequent floodwaters of the Ohio River wrought havoc with the terminals' structures and trackwork. Even when the river did not overflow its banks, passengers were routinely inconvenienced by the lack of efficient connections between stations—a common source of frustration in cities served by multiple terminals. By the late 1920s over 50 interline sleeping cars were being forwarded by Cincinnati's railroads every day, and the lack of a common station made this an expensive and time-consuming task.

What was needed, of course, was a union station able to accommodate the interconnecting passenger trains of each of the city's railroads—and to offer them immunity from the recurring flood threat. Despite efforts to that end, the geography of the city—with its narrow valleys and proximity to the Ohio River—had frustrated advocates of a union terminal until agreement was reached in 1928 to locate a new facility in the Mill Creek valley, approximately two miles west of the city's downtown core and already served by five of Cincinnati's seven railroads. The specific site proposed was occupied by a Southern Railway freight yard, but plans called for this facility to be relocated immediately west of the new terminal. Concerns over the site's susceptibility to flooding were addressed with a plan to raise the grade level of the entire new complex by

approximately 16 feet. Requiring over five million cubic yards of fill, this massive undertaking literally laid the groundwork for Cincinnati Union Terminal. A hill on the west side of Mill Creek, the aptly named Bald Knob, contributed the necessary fill and still exhibits the project's scars.

The Cincinnati Union Terminal Company (CUTCo) was formed in 1927 as a jointly owned property of the seven railroads involved: the "Big Four Route" (New York Central's Cleveland, Cincinnati, Chicago & St. Louis subsidiary); Baltimore & Ohio; the Pennsylvania Railroad; Southern Railway; Louisville & Nashville; Chesapeake & Ohio; and the Norfolk & Western. Officers of CUTCo, its owner railroads, and the Cincinnati Railroad Terminal Development Company formalized the project on June 15, 1929, by placing their signatures on the 42-page "Agreement for Union Station Facilities at Cincinnati."

The architectural firm of Fellheimer & Wagner was commissioned, shortly after completion of their work on Buffalo Central Terminal, to design Cincinnati's new "front door." Although their design for Cincinnati Union Terminal was noted for efficiency and fluidity throughout its track, vehicular, and pedestrian components, the highlight of the complex was its Art Deco head house. Much of the structure's Art Deco mastery can be attributed to designer Paul Cret, whom Fellheimer & Wagner brought into the project at the request of the CUTCo board. The terminal's strong, unadorned geometric forms, at once contrasting and complementary, became an icon of Art Deco design, instantly recognizable as nothing else than Cincinnati Union Terminal. As a railroad terminal and a civic landmark, Fellheimer & Wagner and Cret had created a masterpiece. (Interestingly, Cret would go on to become instrumental in the design of new streamlined trains that would serve many terminals.)

Cincinnati's $8.5-million terminal opened in mid-March 1933, two weeks earlier than planned in order to admit trains flooded out of their soon-to-be-closed stations. CUT could have had no more appropriate a debut.

The terminal's head house was located at the west end of a long landscaped vehicle approach, and faced east toward the necessarily distant city center. The facade took the form of a limestone-clad semi-circular arch flanked by low curved north and south wings that served as a vehicular entrance and exit, respectively. Centered in the arched facade were groups of vertical windows, and in front of these were two stepped pylons supporting a 16-foot diameter, neon-illuminated clock. The station's main entrance, set off by a marquee and the use of dark granite trim, was located at the base of the window arch. It opened through a vestibule into a breathtaking main concourse that took the form of a quarter-sphere. Its 176-foot-wide x 125-foot-deep semicircular terrazzo floor was located under a semi-circular ceiling decorated in pastel shades of yellow and

CUT's pastel-hued rotunda ceiling was suspended within the terminal's larger exterior dome. Winold Reiss' two mosaic murals—each 25 x 105 feet—depicted Cincinnati's development and American history. This view was taken on CUT's final evening of Amtrak service in October 1972.—MIKE SCHAFER

BIRD'S-EYE VIEW OF CINCINNATI, OHIO, UNION TERMINAL IN FOREGROUND

3A-H931

orange and reaching a maximum height of 125 feet. An information kiosk and clock were located near the center of the concourse floor, while the station's 18 ticket windows, lunch room, retail shops, and even a newsreel theater were located around its periphery. Natural light, admitted by the window panels in the front facade, helped illuminate the concourse's sweeping 25 x 105-foot glass mosaics. Executed by artist Winold Reiss, one of these mosaics depicted the evolution of Cincinnati, while the other celebrated American history.

As passengers passed through the main concourse toward the rear of the head house, they entered the terrazzo-floored train concourse, a 78 x 410-foot space above the station's 14 platform tracks. A dozen clusters of semi-circular leather seating accommodated passengers prior to boarding, during which time they could also admire more of Reiss' glass-mosaic murals in this part of the terminal. A

dozen mosaics occupied the walls between the concourse's train gates and depicted Cincinnati industry, while a mosaic map of the U.S. and the globe's eastern and western hemispheres graced the room's west wall. A pair of smaller mosaics, at the extreme east end of the room, were stylized renditions of a steam locomotive and heavyweight open-platform observation car. The gently arched ceiling of the train concourse reflected the same yellow and orange color scheme of the main concourse.

Baggage and express was accommodated on the terminal's lower level, which opened onto grade-level beneath the raised passenger areas. A post-office annex and separate express building were located north of the head house, only two of the terminal complex's total of 22 buildings. Even farther beyond these were the terminal's 26-track coach yard, power house, and engine terminal. As built, the latter featured a 20-stall roundhouse and 17 outdoor tracks, serviced by a 115-foot-diameter turntable. With the exception of the Southern, all of CUT's railroads had their locomotives serviced at this facility, along with the CUTCo's own fleet of switchers.

Train movements within the station area itself were controlled by Tower A, an interlocking plant housed not in a conventional ground-level tower but in a large room integral to the rear of the head house above the east end of the train concourse.

By the time CUT opened in 1933, the passenger traffic it had been built to handle had dropped by almost half. World War II provided it a widely experienced temporary traffic surge—CUT handled its 12-million passenger peak with ease—but the terminal never had the heyday experienced by many of its urban counterparts. It had simply been built too big and too late.

Even before Amtrak inherited the remnants of CUT's once-far-flung schedules, its owners had cast about for ways to relieve themselves of its financial burden. Redevelopment schemes were floated, ranging from conversion of the station to a hotel or new city hall to reinventing it as a prison, but none were pursued at the time.

CUT had the dubious distinction of being the first major station used by Amtrak to be abandoned in favor of one built expressly for the new passenger train operator. After less than 18 months at CUT, Amtrak vacated the terminal on October 28, 1972. Few then would have ever expected Amtrak to return to CUT. Fewer still expected CUT itself to survive, especially after the Southern Railway bought the train concourse end of the building and demolished it to accommodate a piggyback freight yard. Weiss' concourse mosaics were sensitively saved—all but

the map—and relocated for display at Greater Cincinnati Airport, which had usurped CUT as Cincinnati's gateway.

Following several more years of disinterest, the main concourse and its adjacent wings were transformed into an ill-fated retail mall, doomed by the station's progressively seedy environs and an economic downturn in the early 1980s. The terminal's future again looked bleak until two Cincinnati museums considered a redeveloped terminal for their joint expansion. After feasibility studies and and infusion of $33-million in dedicated city tax funds, the terminal's future brightened considerably.

The Cincinnati Historical Society and the Cincinnati Museum of Natural History collaborated to create the Museum Center at Union Terminal, adapting the station's 200,000 square feet of underground parking and ramp space for state-of-the-art exhibits. The main concourse was left unchanged and restored to its original appearance, with the original information kiosk serving as the Museums' ticket desk. Retail space was refurbished, as was the newsreel theater. Even the former Tower A was reopened, this time as an observation area and headquarters of the Cincinnati Railroad Club. The blocked-off entrance to the former train concourse was adapted for use as an Omnimax™ theater. The one-time men's lounge was refurbished as a handsome waiting room/ticket counter, marking Amtrak's return to CUT on July 29, 1991, after an almost 19-year absence, with the tri-weekly Chicago–Washington, D.C., *Cardinal*.

The eastbound first section of New York Central's *Ohio State Limited* departs CUT on July 25, 1948. The boxy structure to the right of the terminal's dome is Tower A, from where CUT's train movements and trackage were controlled.—DICK ACTON SR.

CLEVELAND UNION TERMINAL

This largely subterranean facility formed part of an urban redevelopment incorporating, in its prime, a pre-existing 920-room hotel, a department store, and the 708-foot, 52-story Terminal Tower. Over 1,000 structures were demolished—displacing an estimated 15,000 Clevelanders—to make way for the 104-acre betterment.

The project was spearheaded by two Cleveland brothers, Oris and Mantis Van Sweringen. They were real-estate developers who became involved in rapid transit as a means to connect the affluent residents of their Shaker Heights suburban development with the businesses and stores of downtown Cleveland. Their pragmatic rapid-transit goals were frustrated by a railroad—the New York, Chicago & St. Louis (the "Nickel Plate Road")—that denied the Van Sweringens the use of a small portion of its right-of-way and thereby prevented the suburban line's entry into downtown. The brothers' solution was to secure their needed access in a straightforward if unorthodox manner—they bought the Nickel Plate Road from its then-owner, New York Central, for $8.5 million. NYC had been obliged to seek a buyer in the wake of government anti-trust action, so the arrangement was tailor-made for both parties.

As the Vans (as the brothers were known) developed a taste for big-time railroading, their holdings grew to include such prominent roads as the Chesapeake & Ohio, Erie, and Pere Marquette, in addition to the NKP. Their desire for a suitable headquarters and mounting civic pressure for the NYC to replace its obsolete 1864 lakefront depot coalesced into the Terminal Tower complex on Cleveland's Public Square.

Earlier unrealized proposals for a new union station had centered on Cleveland's civic center (later known as the Mall), a manifestation of Daniel Burnham's City Beautiful esthetic that stretched from Superior Avenue north toward Lake Erie and the NYC's main line. Burnham's 1903 Group Plan, most of which was implemented, included provision for a monumental and never-built Beaux-Arts railroad terminal at the north end of his civic center. Design proposals for the lakefront station were being undertaken as late as 1917, but America's entry into World War I effectively killed the project.

A union station on the city's Public Square came to pass as a result of the Vans' tenacity in promoting the interests of their own rapid-transit and rail holdings, and their relationship with New York Central's Alfred H. Smith. Smith had surreptitiously facilitated the brothers' 1916 purchase of the Nickel Plate, and in 1918, as a director of the wartime United States Railroad Administration, he urged the brothers to expand their proposed Public Square terminal to accommodate trains that would otherwise use the stalled lakefront station. Seeing the wisdom—and

On June 18, 1947, one of Cleveland Union Terminal's P-1a-class 2-C+C-2 electrics wheeled St. Louis-bound Nickel Plate Road train 9 west out of the terminal toward the Cuyahoga River viaduct. When CUT's electrification was shut down in 1953, the 21 surviving "P-motors" moved east to work out of New York's Grand Central Terminal.—RICHARD J. COOK, ALLEN COUNTY HISTORICAL SOCIETY COLLECTION

profitability—of Smith's idea, the Vans found themselves in a position to finally give Cleveland its union station.

Cleveland Union Terminal was designed by the firm of Graham, Anderson, Probst & White, a Chicago architectural partnership that had submitted earlier proposals for the stillborn lakefront union station. Owned by the Cleveland Union Terminals Company (which was, in turn, owned 93 percent by NYC and 7 percent by NKP), Cleveland Union Terminal opened on June 28, 1930, just as the Depression was gaining momentum. Terminal Tower, executed as a much taller landmark than had been proposed to the Vans in 1919, had been occupied since 1928. The portion of the complex devoted to rail service included separate "steam" railroad and rapid-transit concourses, a marble-sheathed waiting room, retail stores, and a Fred Harvey restaurant. The steam concourse, located at the extreme rear of the station complex, enjoyed natural light provided by skylights. The station shared its five-arched main entrance with Terminal Tower. Both were reached from Public Square through a 34 x 152-foot portico. Ramps at each end of this portico led to either the Hotel Cleveland or Higbee's Department Store, both of which flanked the tower as integral parts of the complex. Passengers continuing beyond this area found themselves either in Terminal Tower's lobby or in the station, which, at its peak, was served by the trains of four railroads: owners

Union Station and Soldiers' and Sailors' Monument, Cleveland, Ohio

NYC and NKP along with tenants Baltimore & Ohio (after 1934) and Erie (after 1949). The Chesapeake & Ohio Railway, which did not serve Cleveland, nonetheless maintained its corporate headquarters in Terminal Tower as a legacy of the C&O's Van Sweringen control. C&O passenger equipment, in the form of through sleeping cars and official "business" cars, did have a limited presence in the terminal, reaching CUT in the consists of both NYC and (for a time) NKP scheduled trains.

An important aspect of the terminal's construction, particularly from Smith's perspective, was that Cleveland's railroad track congestion be reduced—if not eliminated—wherever possible. As a result, the CUT project involved the construction not just of the station and tower, but of 17 miles of grade-separated dedicated passenger train right-of-way stretching from Collinwood in the east to Linndale on the west. Trains operating west of the station crossed the broad Cuyahoga River valley on a massive new 3,450-foot viaduct. The Vans' use of air rights above the station's 12 underground platform tracks precluded the use of steam locomotives, so the entire CUT main line and station complex was electrified. Nickel Plate and New York Central engine crews handed their trains over to CUT crews at the east and west ends of the terminal district (which, for the NKP, were at East 37th Street and West 38th Street), and the steam locomotives then typically ran "light" on bypass routes to rejoin their train on the opposite side of the city. A fleet of 22 class P-1a electric locomotives, all lettered for Cleveland Union Terminal, pulled trains through the terminal district. As was the case in Buffalo, the NYC's flagship *20th Century Limited* did not

ABOVE: **At 52 stories, Terminal Tower was Cleveland's tallest building for decades. Illuminated at night, it was visible for miles. This postcard view looks across Public Square, with the Hotel Cleveland at right and Higbee's department store at left.**—MIKE SCHAFER COLLECTION

LEFT: **This mid-1920s view recorded progress on Terminal Tower; construction of Higbee's (opened in 1931, to the east of the Tower's base) had yet to commence. The quintet of arches facing Public Square provided access to both the Tower and Union Terminal. The Hotel Cleveland had opened in 1918. At its zenith, the Terminal Tower complex also comprised Cleveland's main Post Office (1934) and the Prospect Buildings, a trio of office blocks (the Republic, Guildhall, and Midland Buildings) opened at Prospect Avenue and Ontario Street between 1928 and 1930.**—JOHN B. CORNS COLLECTION

the electric motors' wake, CUT still provided switching service for its occupants with a small group of CUT-lettered General Motors switchers and road-switchers.

Like Buffalo and Cincinnati—both opened at the outset of the Depression—Cleveland Union Terminal never had the chance to perform to its full potential. The Nickel Plate's modest use of the terminal ended in September 1965 with the discontinuance of a final Buffalo–Chicago daytime schedule less than a year after NKP itself had become part of the Norfolk & Western Railway. When Amtrak's brief occupancy of CUT ended, only an Erie Lackawanna (later Conrail) commuter schedule to Youngstown, Ohio, remained—a vestige of the former Erie operation.

Cleveland Union Terminal retained a rapid-transit presence after its last intercity train departed. Those former platform tracks not required for light-rail service were paved over and used as a parking lot, as was the former coach yard at the rear of the terminal. Much of the interior spaces originally built to serve rail passengers were redeveloped in the 1980s and early 1990s when Terminal Tower was recast as Tower City, an upscale retail and dining venue with an animated indoor fountain as its centerpiece. Following its early withdrawal, Amtrak returned to Cleveland—ironically serving the city from a small station not far from the site of the 1864 lakefront depot.

DETROIT
Michigan Central Station

Like its New York Central compatriot in Buffalo, Detroit's Michigan Central Station survived the departure of its last passenger train only to become a forlorn monument—impressive from afar, but under close scrutiny a depressing, broken hulk.

Construction of the Beaux-Arts complex began in 1912, in conjunction with overall terminal improvements undertaken by Michigan Central following completion of the Detroit River Tunnel in 1910. The new twin-tube tunnel replaced a cumbersome carferry arrangement and gave the railroad quick and direct access to its former Canada Southern main line across southern Ontario to Buffalo.

The new terminal's design was a collaborative effort of two architectural partnerships, Reed & Stem and Warren & Wetmore. Both had family ties to the New York Central System, of which the Michigan Central Railroad was a key component. When it opened on December 27, 1913, MC Station replaced the railroad's small Romanesque terminal at Jefferson and Third streets in Detroit. The new terminal was located a short distance from the tunnel's American portal, and its station and approach tracks were electrified to eliminate the risks associated with smoke in the tunnel. Electric locomotives piloted trains through the bore between the station and Windsor on the Canadian side. As

This July 1950 view, looking north past Terminal Tower and Public Square, shows a portion of the New York Central coach yard, at lower left. The square skylight-capped structure surrounded by parking provided access to CUT's "steam concourse," so-named to differentiate its intercity trains from the rapid transit services also serving the terminal.—BRUCE YOUNG COLLECTION

serve CUT. Instead, the *Century* bypassed the terminal completely, never leaving the NYC's lakefront main line.

As diesels replaced steam locomotives as road power on the passenger trains through CUT, the need for a dedicated fleet of electric locomotives and their power-supply infrastructure was lessened—so much so that CUT's electrified operations were discontinued on November 16, 1953. While diesel exhaust proved a moderate nuisance as it wafted up from the depths of the station, the expense of electrification—at least in Cleveland—was too much to justify. In

would later be the case in Buffalo and Cincinnati, the railway's physical plant dictated that the station be located a moderate distance from the downtown area—in Detroit, the "convenience gap" dictated by the tunnel's location was about one and a half miles.

The architects' plans included a park that would serve as the station's "front lawn." The understandable resistance of property owners residing on the site of the proposed park delayed commencement of its construction until 1918. Upon opening in 1922, the landscaped space was named Roosevelt Park in honor of the late president.

The 262 x 345-foot x 76-foot-tall station's facade was dominated by a trio of soaring arched windows, evocative of New York's Grand Central Terminal on which the two architectural firms had also worked. Immediately inside the entrance was the station's 104 x 233-foot main waiting room, with a women's waiting room, restaurants, shops, and ticket office scattered around its edges. A ticket lobby connected the main waiting room with the 78 x 193-foot skylight-capped concourse. The ticket lobby and concourse could also be entered through an arcade on the building's east side that served a city streetcar loop until 1938.

A 1,100-foot-long Bush train shed sheltered the station's ten platform tracks, which were accessible from the concourse gates via a gently sloped underground ramp and staircases. A 175-car coach yard and related car servicing structures were located northwest of the station. Steam, electric (and, later, diesel) locomotives were serviced at a nearby MC facility.

Michigan Central Station shared more than a depressing fate with its 1929 opposite number at the east end of Lake Erie—both terminals incorporated prominent office towers. While Buffalo's was a sculpted Art Deco pylon, Detroit's reflected its earlier origin and took the boxy form of a somewhat stunted 15-story skyscraper. In fact, the dominating mass of Detroit's office tower looming over the station presaged a similar

MICHIGAN CENTRAL STATION, DETROIT, MICH.

ENTRANCE TO DETROIT RIVER TUNNEL.

LEFT: While Michigan Central Station's Beaux-Arts head house bore a resemblance to New York's Grand Central Terminal—they were designed by the same architects—it was overpowered by an integrated office tower. The American portals of the twin-tube Detroit River Tunnel were located a short distance from MC Station, and had weighed heavily on the site choice for the new terminal. The tunnel gave the New York Central's "Great Steel Fleet" quick access to the former Canada Southern route across Southern Ontario to Buffalo and points east.—MIKE SCHAFER COLLECTION

BELOW: Michigan Central depot was in its final years as a railroad terminal when the inside main entrance was photographed during the 1977 Christmas holiday season.—MIKE SCHAFER

waiting room in 1975 (it had been closed by NYC in 1967) and resurrecting passenger service through the tunnel and across Ontario to Buffalo for a time. Amtrak vacated the terminal in January 1988, a decade after $1.25 million in improvements failed to stem MC Station's decline. Urban blight had figured largely in Amtrak's decision and steadily overtook the station's surroundings. After Conrail, the corporate successor to NYC and Penn Central, vacated its tower offices and storage space in 1987, the inexorable forces of neglect and vandalism moved in. The Bush train shed was razed in October 1999, leaving the station and tower to await their fate amid a growing public awareness of the terminal's plight.

Fort Street Union Depot

Closer to the Detroit River, Fort Street Union Depot hosted trains of the Pere Marquette (PM, merged into the Chesapeake & Ohio in 1947), Wabash, and Pennsylvania Railroads. Fort Street's history went back to 1892 when the Wabash, the Flint & Pere Marquette (PM's predecessor), and Canadian Pacific cooperated to establish a joint terminal. The new terminal was opened on January 21, 1893. The PRR replaced Canadian Pacific in the triumvirate of owners, which controlled the Fort Street Union Depot Company (FSUD) through its jointly held Union Belt Railroad of Detroit subsidiary.

The Romanesque structure was located at Third and Fort streets. The three-story head house occupied an area of 118 x 166 feet, with an adjoining 311-foot-long, two-story wing along Fort Street. A 100-foot-tall clock tower loomed over the head house. In order to appease adjoining property owners, the station's approach tracks were carried above Fort Street on a 15-block-long double-track steel viaduct, promptly nicknamed the "High Line," which reached grade at 18th Street.

Terminal switching was handled by FSUD's own locomotives, including a pair of rare General Motors NW5s acquired in 1947. Trains due for departure typically backed along the viaduct and into the station behind an FSUD switch locomotive prior to boarding. Empty trains were removed from the station in the same manner, while Wabash and Pere Marquette road crews moved their own "light" locomotives into and out of the station. In the PRR's case, however, the High Line viaduct was not strong enough to accommodate the railroad's subsequently developed heavy K-4 Pacific locomotives. Occupied PRR trains therefore had the distinction of being moved into and out of the station by FSUD switchers which traded places with a K-4 at 18th Street.

In its prime, Fort Street Union Depot handled almost 30 trains each day. The station's wartime traffic peak occurred in 1944 when over 1.5 million travelers used its facilities, but by 1959 the PRR had called it quits when it

The Detroit leg of Chesapeake & Ohio's Virginia-bound *Sportsman* departs Detroit's Fort Street Union Depot in 1956. The terminal's Richardsonian Romanesque head house is visible just beyond the platform canopies. At the time of this view, trains of the Wabash and Pennsylvania railroads also called at Fort Street.—C&O HISTORICAL SOCIETY COLLECTION

juxtaposition involving the architects' Grand Central Terminal, which was overshadowed by the Pan Am Building after 1963.

In its heyday, MC Station served trains of tenants Baltimore & Ohio and Canadian Pacific, in addition to the Great Steel Fleet of landlord New York Central (Michigan Central). Mirroring the change in Cleveland, Detroit's electrification ended in 1953 after diesels had essentially eliminated the problem of noxious smoke in the tunnel.

Like its counterparts across the U.S., MC Station fell on hard times as highway and airline travel took away its livelihood. NYC offered the station for sale in 1956, but the $5-million asking price proved too high. Amtrak dutifully moved in on May 1, 1971, even reopening the main

discontinued its *Red Arrow* to northern Michigan. That same year, one of the unusual NW5 switchers was sold, with the second following in 1962. The C&O became the sole FSUD owner in the terminal's final years. Wabash, meanwhile, became part of the Norfolk & Western Railroad in October 1964. These two remaining station occupants soldiered on until 1971, when the facility was made redundant and closed with the creation of Amtrak. Less than three years later, in January 1974, Fort Street Union Depot was razed.

MILWAUKEE

In a city as rich in European heritage as Milwaukee, it is hardly surprising that the foremost two of the city's four rail terminals shared a pronounced Old World flavor. Architecturally, they were as much products of their times as they were throwbacks to the city's heritage. Their shared Romanesque style was at its zenith when the two terminals were created for the city's two most prominent railroads, the Chicago, Milwaukee & St. Paul ("The Milwaukee Road") and the Chicago & North Western.

This November 1935 view of Milwaukee Road's Everett Street Depot looks eastward in the railroad's namesake city. The Public Service Building—The Milwaukee Electric Railway & Light Company's interurban and streetcar terminal—lies just beyond the Milwaukee station's Romanesque head house.—MILWAUKEE ROAD, COURTESY JIM STAROSTA

Nov. 14-1935.

The streamlined handiwork of industrial designer Otto Kuhler is apparent in this late-1940s view of the Milwaukee Road's hometown terminal, looking east from North 5th Street. At far left, Atlantic No. 4 is on train 29 for Madison, Wisconsin. The middle train, with a Hudson, is on the combined *North Woods Hiawatha* and *Chippewa-Hiawatha*. Pacific 151 at right is waiting to take the *Chippewa-Hiawatha* on to Green Bay and points north. It is sitting with cars—filled with passengers who have already boarded—originating at Milwaukee for Green Bay and north.—PHOTOGRAPHER UNKNOWN, DAVE INGLES COLLECTION

Everett Street Depot

Milwaukee Union Station opened in 1886 and was home to the trains of the city's namesake railroad, the Chicago, Milwaukee & St. Paul, as well as those of the Wisconsin Central (a future component of the Soo Line) and Milwaukee Northern (a future component of the Milwaukee Road). The station's most famous occupants were the *Hiawathas*, a harvest-hued streamlined counterpoint to the station's dark stone formality.

The terminal was located at the heart of the city in an area bounded by North 2nd Street on the east, North 5th Street on the west, West Everett Street and Fourth Ward Park on the north, and West Clybourn Street on the south. The head house fronted Everett Street, hence the facility's more commonly known name, Everett Street Depot, though to many it was simply the "Milwaukee Road Depot." The Romanesque head house was flanked on its east side by a mail building and on the west by a Railway Express facility. After the turn of the twentieth century, Everett Street had two close neighbor terminals: across the

street to the northeast, the Public Service Building, which served as the main terminal of the sprawling The Milwaukee Electric Railway & Light Company (the "TM"); and a block west the terminal of high-speed Chicago–Milwaukee interurban Chicago North Shore & Milwaukee.

Everett Street Depot's through tracks paralleled West Clybourn Street and in fact crossed the thoroughfare twice as they curved into and out of the train shed—a liability throughout the day considering the number of through trains, Chicago–Milwaukee corridor runs, and Milwaukee–Madison and other local trains that constantly paraded in and out of the station. A classic inverted "V" train shed sheltered entraining and detraining passengers.

The passenger area of the depot head house was remodeled twice during its 79-year life, the second time with an Indian-themed décor that nicely complemented The Milwaukee Road's signature streamliners, the *Hiawatha*s. However, the station's inevitable decline was marked by—for structural reasons—the shortening of the clock tower in 1953.

On August 4, 1965, the Milwaukee Road shifted its passenger train operations to a modernistic, if somewhat stark, new terminal built—at the behest of the city—two blocks south at West St. Paul Avenue and 5th Street. The following year, Everett Street Depot was leveled.

North Western Station

Chicago & North Western's Milwaukee station was built in 1889 at the eastern edge of downtown, overlooking Lake Michigan. Arguably less ponderous and brooding than Milwaukee Road's Everett Street Depot, North Western Station was a solidly built brick-and-stone facility featuring a prominent tower that became a landmark of the city's waterfront.

As with the Milwaukee Road facility, North Western Station was home to a wide array of through trains. From the stately lakefront terminal passengers could board trains direct to Minneapolis/St. Paul, Duluth, Green Bay (via two routes), Madison, Upper Michigan, and northern Wisconsin. The depot was also the north-end anchor to a number of Chicago–Milwaukee corridor trains. Like its cross-town contemporary, the North Western Station hosted a latter-day fleet of lightweight streamlined trains—the green-and-yellow *"400s"*—that couldn't help but draw

This aerial view looks eastward in the late 1950s and illustrates how tracks crossed West Clybourn Street twice to reach the Milwaukee Road terminal's train shed. The coach yard is partially visible at the bottom of the photo— there were storage tracks at the depot as well, usually used for consists stored intact. The North Shore interurban terminal can be seen at lower left, with tracks approaching off the 6th Street bridge.—ROBERT T. MC COY PHOTO, COURTESY NATE MOLLDREM

ABOVE: This February 1964 time exposure looks southward at the C&NW Milwaukee depot on the city's lakefront. Lake Michigan lies just beyond the left edge of the photograph. A member of the North Western's *"400"* fleet is laying over for the night.—BOB BULLERMANN

LEFT: Interior views of the C&NW's Milwaukee station are rare. This is how it appeared in the spring of 1966—its final year of operation—with rental lockers and streamlined trash containers the only detractions from the structure's baronial flavor.—BOB BULLERMANN

attention to the fact that the Romanesque building was of another era. In due time, society would see that as an attribute, but in the 1950s and 1960s it was a distinct liability. The lakeside terminal handled its last train in 1966, and what could have become a revered front-yard landmark for the city was subsequently demolished in favor of expanded parking facilities. C&NW's remaining passenger trains moved to the new Milwaukee Road station that had opened the previous year.

Milwaukee Road Depot II

Just as Milwaukee's two "classic" terminals reflected the strong Romanesque tastes of their day, the Milwaukee Road's 1965 station—the last urban passenger terminal built for private railroad use in the U.S.—was very much a product of its time. It was a sterile denouncement of its two Romanesque predecessors. Milwaukee's new station exhibited a futuristic form, reflective of the minimalist tastes then in vogue, which nonetheless managed to evoke through its recurring arches elements of the Beaux Arts movement popular five decades earlier. Even that favorite adornment of the Romanesque architect—the clock

tower—was reinvented, this time as a somewhat spindly bell tower (with an electronic bell that never quite sounded right) that would have been equally at home in a modernistic church.

Dedicated on August 3, 1965, the new terminal was designed by the Milwaukee architectural firm of Donald L. Grieb & Associates. It also served trains of the Chicago & North Western—though a "union station" appellation never stuck—and housed Milwaukee Road general offices, including dispatching facilities. C&NW was to move its general offices to the building as well, but never did.

The city continued to rely on its new station as Amtrak assumed operation of most of the country's passenger trains in 1971. Long-anticipated renovation plans for the 34-year old structure were formalized in 1999, with the $4-million project expected to reach completion in late 2001. While preserving the station's exterior, new pedestrian flow and interior spaces would be created for the station's users, now approaching a half million per year. New interior décor was to mimic the classic *Hiawatha* theming of yore, with an Art Deco touch and including an aptly named "Hiawatha" restaurant.

The C&NW's northbound *Flambeau "400"* departs Milwaukee's new station for Green Bay and Ashland, Wisconsin, in 1967. The crane in the background marks the construction of a new Post Office building over the station's eastern throat tracks. The Milwaukee Road cars at left are in the coach yard, part of which survived from the old Everett Street station. Just over a week after the new station opened, its Milwaukee Road predecessor was badly damaged by fire.—BOB BULLERMANN

St. Louis Union Station

This mammoth terminal opened on September 1, 1894, and traced its origins to the formation of the Terminal Railroad Association of St. Louis (TRRA) five years earlier. The TRRA had been established by a group of six St. Louis railroads to act as an impartial operator of joint terminal facilities, including the Eads and Merchants bridges across the Mississippi River. Much of this infrastructure had been under the control of financier Jay Gould, and the TRRA was successful in breaking what had amounted to a terminal monopoly.

Among the first orders of business for the newly formed TRRA was the replacement of the city's existing Union Depot, a facility which had opened in 1870 and had long since been outgrown. St. Louis architect Theodore C. Link was awarded the commission—and a $10,000 prize—to design St. Louis' new $6.5-million Union Station in 1892. The 80 x 606-foot head house was executed in the Romanesque style that would begin to fall from public favor just as the new station opened, with architects moving to embrace the Beaux Arts trends popularized by the 1893 Columbian Exposition in Chicago. Unlike most of its Romanesque contemporaries, which were typically dark structures of red or brown stone, St. Louis Union Station thankfully incorporated light-colored Indiana limestone.

Between the head house and 32-track train shed, Link provided the 70 x 606-foot "Midway"—essentially a concourse open to the train shed—through which the wrought-iron train gates were reached from the head house. The station's Market Street frontage was highlighted

BELOW: St. Louis Union Station, in a westward view along Market Street in 1986.—MIKE SCHAFER

INSET: The famous allegorical stained-glass window showing New York, St. Louis, and San Francisco was photographed in 1970.—MIKE SCHAFER

by a 230-foot clock tower. Inside the head house, travelers could avail themselves of lodging (at the aptly named Terminal Hotel), a Fred Harvey restaurant, and various retail outlets in addition to facilities devoted to ticketing, baggage handling, and railroad offices.

The 32 original platform tracks were all stub-ended, making St. Louis Union Station a true terminal by the strictest definition. Arriving trains routinely backed in, which had the double benefit of placing cars occupied by passengers closest to the head house, and keeping the smoke, noise, and bustle of the train's head end (with its locomotive and mail, baggage, and express cars) removed from the passengers as much as practical. There were a few exceptions to the back-in routine, including some Missouri Pacific commuter runs, Illinois Central's *Green Diamond* articulated trainset of the late 1930s, some short diesel-powered trains of the late pre-Amtrak era, and Amtrak's double-ended Turboliners.

Only a decade after it opened, St. Louis Union Station was called upon to support an event for which the terminal's unprecedented capacity was nonetheless inadequate. The 1904 World's Fair put St. Louis on the world map, and Union Station and much of the TRRA's related infrastructure was expanded and upgraded to accommodate the projected crowds. Ten additional platform tracks were installed, under umbrella sheds, in the "Garden" just west of the train shed. The shed itself and platform tracks were extended, and 35 freight elevators facilitated the handling of baggage, mail, and express to

and from trackside via new underground tunnels. The TRRA eliminated a major source of congestion by establishing locomotive-servicing facilities a few blocks east of the station. Prior to this change, such moves routinely crossed the Mississippi to reach service facilities in Illinois, and even after the TRRA facilities opened, a handful of cost-conscious railroads still maintained their own locomotives east of the river. All switching moves into and out of the station were handled by TRRA locomotives and crews.

Feeding the 32 tracks from the train shed to the TRRA main line, which ran east-west perpendicular to the station tracks' orientation, required some ingenious and complex trackwork, also beefed up for the Fair. The train-shed tracks were effectively divided into two groups of 16, each of which was connected to the TRRA main line via a three-track "wye." The density of the train-shed tracks dictated that one leg of each of the two resulting wyes overlapped, creating the "grand crossing" where the wye tracks intersected. Movements were controlled by nearby interlocking towers, the most important of which—Tower 1—sat adjacent to the grand crossing. Despite (or, perhaps, because of) its complexity, the station's track plan was remarkably fluid. The proof of this is particularly evident in the traffic figures related to the 1904 Fair. In the years prior to and after the Fair, the station typically handled between 250 and 290 train movements per day. During the Fair this figure almost doubled. During 1903, the station processed nearly 1.5 million pieces of baggage. Through the Fair year of 1904, this figure ballooned to almost 2.4 million.

Trackside at St. Louis Union Station, looking northwesterly in late 1964. That's the GM&O's northbound *Abraham Lincoln* leaving the station as the IC's *Chickasaw* (serving as the Carbondale–St. Louis connection for the *Panama Limited* and *Seminole* as well) backs in. A solitary Burlington E-unit waits in the background, having just arrived on the *Zephyr Rocket* from Minneapolis. Just visible at left are the nine diamonds of the terminal's "grand crossing," the point at which the pair of three-track "wye" leads serving the train shed intersected.—ALAN BRADLEY

St. Louis Union Station's Grand Hall. The allegorical stained-glass window shown on page 62 is just out of this view at left, in the staircase.—PHIL AND BEV BIRK COLLECTION

Postwar improvements to Union Station's passenger facilities included this decidedly modern-looking ticket counter, photographed on August 4, 1966.—MIKE SCHAFER

As an American railroad center, St. Louis was second only to Chicago. In terms of passenger terminals, St. Louis eclipsed its counterpart on Lake Michigan—whereas the Windy City's 20 passenger trunk lines were scattered among six major terminals, St. Louis Union Station alone was served, in its heyday, by an unrivaled 22 railroads—more than any other single terminal in the world.

(Nonetheless, St. Louis Union was not the only rail terminal in St. Louis. From 1931 to 1958, interurban railway Illinois Terminal boasted an imposing seven-story terminal building for its intercity and suburban services. The modernistic structure today serves as headquarters for the St. Louis *Globe-Democrat*.) Even as railroads consolidated, St. Louis Union Station still boasted a remarkable 16 railroads on the eve of World War II, in addition to owner TRRA.

On July 22, 1940, a three-alarm fire destroyed Tower 1. What could have been a crippling situation was circumvented by $2^1/_2$ months of manual track control before a new interlocking system and Tower 1 structure were completed and opened on October 8, 1940. Befitting its importance, the new interlocking plant—purchased in desperation from an accommodating Pennsylvania Railroad—was dedicated on November 30, 1940, in the presence of New York *Herald-Tribune* columnist and pioneer rail enthusiast Lucius Beebe. That same year a much more esthetic note was recorded in the station's history, as sculptor Carl Milles' *Meeting of the Waters* fountain was installed facing the station's Market Street frontage.

The expansion and improvements of 1904—as well as the brand-new Tower 1—served St. Louis Union Station admirably during World War II. In 1943, the station averaged 199 train movements and just over 1,800 cars per day. Over the course of that year, approximately 22 million passengers passed through the terminal.

The kaleidoscope of railroads serving St. Louis Union Station was never more colorful that it was during the height of the streamliner era following World War II, when brightly painted and marvelously equipped lightweight trains fought what proved to be a losing battle for the traveling public's attention. On any given day, the best and the brightest that America's railroads had to offer could be seen at St. Louis Union.

Unfortunately, the best wasn't good enough to stem the nationwide flow of passengers from trains to automobiles and aircraft. As the 1950s gave way to the 1960s, St. Louis Union Station was a particularly depressing showcase of what passenger rail service in the U.S. had become, with progressively fewer trains echoing within a decaying facility. Seven railroads had vacated the station during the 1950s, and on the eve of Amtrak in early 1971 only seven remained: Illinois Central; the affiliated Baltimore & Ohio/Chesapeake & Ohio; Gulf, Mobile & Ohio; Louisville & Nashville; Penn Central; Norfolk & Western; and Missouri Pacific. Collectively, they offered a dozen daily trains to and from the terminal. Those few passengers venturing inside the station in 1971 found that the Terminal Hotel and Fred Harvey restaurant had been closed. In perhaps the ultimate humiliation, the station's throat tracks were vaulted by Interstate 40's elevated roadway.

Amtrak came to St. Louis in May 1971 in the form of two Chicago–St. Louis trains and a through Kansas City–New York run. Remarkably, the latter was the first scheduled through-train service in the station's history. Despite introducing new route and services via St. Louis through the mid-1970s, Amtrak could not justify the continued occupancy of such a cavernous terminal. In October 1978, Amtrak moved its operations out of Union Station to a nearby "temporary" facility still in use today.

Just five months after Amtrak's departure, St. Louis Union Station was purchased by Oppenheimer Properties as a prelude to a $135 million redevelopment. The structure was restored, hotel accommodation was reintroduced under Hyatt Regency management, and 160,000 square feet of retail space was created in the head house, Midway, and portions of the train shed.

The newly redeveloped Union Station complex was a smash hit with the public, and it instantly became—and remains—one of the top tourist destinations in the Midwest. With the 1990s came St. Louis' new light-rail system, whose route (aside from using the TRRA's former city tunnel to get through downtown from Eads Bridge) passes under—and stopped at—Union Station, making possible quick trips to Union Station for lunch for downtown business people. Unfortunately, Union Station management shunned suggestions of Amtrak returning to the station via the Garden tracks, which are still in place and used by occasional special-train moves, and as of the close of the twentieth century, Amtrak continued to await action from the city to develop a new transportation terminal.

Union Station Midway, St. Louis, Mo.

St. Louis Union Station's 70 x 606-foot Midway as it appeared around the turn of the twentieth century. This view looks west from the east-side staircase. The station's cavernous balloon-roofed train shed is at left, separated from the Midway by cast-iron gates.—PHIL AND BEV BIRK COLLECTION

With the smells of coal smoke and diesel exhaust having been replaced by the more palatable aromas of baked goods and coffee, this is how the Midway appeared in 1986 after Union Station's redevelopment, in a view duplicating the vantage point of the postcard above.—MIKE SCHAFER

4 CHICAGO: THE CROSSROADS

- • DEARBORN STATION • CENTRAL STATION
- • GRAND CENTRAL STATION • LA SALLE STREET STATION
- • NORTH WESTERN TERMINAL • UNION STATION
- • JOLIET UNION STATION

Chicago was, and to a great extent still is, the heart of the North American rail industry. Railroads and suppliers alike located their headquarters in the Windy City. In suburban LaGrange, General Motors' Electro-Motive Division did more than any other company to transform the nation's railroads from steam-powered to diesel-powered enterprises. On the south side of the city, equipment for some of the most luxurious passenger trains in the land rolled out of the Pullman-Standard Car Manufacturing Company.

The sheer number of railroads serving the city in the industry's post-World War II heyday—over 20 trunk lines, as well as terminal and transfer companies and shortlines—were at once a blessing and a curse. Traffic volume and converging routes around the south end of Lake Michigan created bottlenecks for freight traffic, while an intransigent blend of corporate vanity, fiscal pragmatism, geography, and politics gave Chicago an unrivaled six major passenger terminals through

ABOVE: For some 45 years, the Elgin clock on the east side facade of Chicago Union Station's concourse building provided a reminder of just how many minutes travelers had until train time.—MIKE SCHAFER

LEFT: A mere two blocks north of Union Station, North Western Terminal served trains and passengers of the Chicago & North Western. On July 19, 1979, a trio of afternoon commuter trains—still wearing the colors of the C&NW's famed *"400"* streamliners—congregated at the curve just north of the terminal.—JOE MC MILLAN

Reflecting the terminal's original name of Polk Street Depot, this postcard depicts Dearborn Street Station's appearance before a 1922 fire shortened the tower and eliminated the steeply pitched head-house roofs. A third story was later added between the tower and each corner block.
—KEVIN HOLLAND COLLECTION

most of the twentieth century. While smaller cities like Cincinnati and New Orleans were able to consolidate their pre-Amtrak passenger trains in a single union station, Chicago—despite a stated desire as late as the 1940s—never did.

To make matters worse, Chicago anchored the "invisible barrier" that separated Eastern railroads from their Western counterparts. Freight traffic moved—sometimes slowly—through the city as cars were interchanged between Eastern and Western lines. Railroads like the Elgin, Joliet & Eastern made the forwarding of freight cars *around* Chicago—as opposed to through it—their stock in trade.

Passengers, on the other hand—as industry gadfly Robert R. Young gleefully jibed in his infamous 1946 "hog" advertisement—could not travel through Chicago without at least a change of trains (hogs could pass through Chicago without changing cars), regardless of whether they were traveling just a few hundred miles or across the country. For the truly intrepid—or unfortunate—a change of station was also involved, although this was made less of a burden if travelers availed themselves of the Parmelee Company's free limousine transfer service. Chicago's invisible barrier was broken briefly in the 1950s as railroads offered through sleeping cars on selected trains in response to Young's taunting—but coach passengers were still out of luck. Travelers who remained aboard their sleeping car as it traveled "through" Chicago—the convenience of which, after all, was the main attraction of the exercise—still were obliged to endure an often rough-riding and invariably time-consuming transfer, this time at the hands of a

switching crew as their transcontinental sleeper was shuttled between stations.

Right up until Amtrak began operating most remaining intercity passenger trains in May 1971, Chicago boasted six major terminals: Central Station, Dearborn Station, La Salle Street Station, Grand Central, Union Station, and North Western Terminal. Three minor terminals were Illinois Central's Randolph Street Station (still operating); Chicago, North Shore & Milwaukee's Roosevelt Road station; and Chicago, Aurora & Elgin's Wells Street Terminal.

Sporadic through cars notwithstanding, Young's barrier wasn't truly punctured until November 14, 1971, when Amtrak initiated two through Milwaukee–St. Louis schedules—the *Prairie State* and an extended *Abraham Lincoln*—as the first scheduled passenger trains to operate through Chicago (a handy arrangement that has since been abolished). The following year, Amtrak consolidated all of its Windy City trains into Union Station, at least in part fulfilling the city's decades-long vision of a single union station. Nonetheless, downtown Chicago still boasts three major (and one minor) terminals as Metra suburban trains continue to serve La Salle Street Station, the former North Western Terminal, Union Station, and Randolph Street.

DEARBORN STATION

Designed by New York architect Cyrus L. W. Eidlitz and opened to traffic on May 8, 1885, Dearborn—originally known as Polk Street Depot—was the longest-serving of Chicago's six major passenger terminals. Appropriately, Dearborn's head house survives as the city's only extant nineteenth century station structure. The red-brick Romanesque building, with its pink granite base and terra cotta detailing, anchors "Printer's Row" and South Dearborn Street at the intersection of its erstwhile namesake, West Polk Street. The station's original steep dormered roofs—including that of the clock tower with its decidedly Flemish overtones—disappeared in the wake of a 1922 fire that left the truncated tower looming over a flat-roofed head house. The station's street-side facade assumed its latter-day appearance when a nondescript third story was inserted adjacent to the base of the tower.

Until its closure after the arrival of Amtrak in 1971, Dearborn hosted Chicago's most cosmopolitan collection of passenger train operations and operators. More railroads called at Dearborn than at any of Chicago's other passenger terminals—seven out of the city's 20 passenger-carrying steam railroads served Dearborn in its postwar heyday—an irony considering Dearborn was the smallest of the big six.

Dearborn's stalwarts spanned geography and social strata alike, with the Santa Fe's legendary *Chief*s and *Super Chief* rubbing shoulders on the station's nine platform

Commencing its 999-mile journey to Hoboken, New Jersey, Erie Lackawanna's *Lake Cities* departs the confines of Dearborn Station on a fall morning in 1966. At lower right in photo, which was taken from the Roosevelt Road overpass, is the roof of the control tower; the loudspeaker was used to bark commands to switchmen on the ground. Note at left in the background, the tower of B&O's Grand Central Station.—MIKE SCHAFER

Crowds mill about Santa Fe's combined *Super Chief/El Capitan* during the early stages of the boarding process at Dearborn Station on a July evening in 1970. Long, gleaming transcontinental streamliners made for an incongruous scenario at stubby little Dearborn. Aside from being hampered by short platform tracks, a modest-size head house, and a street passing through the middle of the station, the tracks at the throat of the station were constricted by the Roosevelt Road overpass (in background), sometimes requiring long trains to be split onto two tracks for boarding and then "doubled" out of the station upon departure.—JIM HEUER

a steam generator in its H12-44 switcher model to create the H12-44TS. The only three such locomotives built—Santa Fe Nos. 541–543—were Dearborn regulars in the company of C&WI's green-and-yellow Alco road-switchers. One of the Santa Fe trio, No. 543, was preserved at the California State Railroad Museum in Sacramento.

Mail and express—as well as commuter services provided by Wabash, C&EI, GTW, and C&WI—were accommodated at an annex built just east of the station in 1914 and intended to reduce congestion at the main terminal. Little known is the fact that two streets passed right through Dearborn Station. Taylor Street cut east and west through the platform tracks while Plymouth Court separated the main part of the station from the Annex. The Annex approach tracks sliced right through the intersection of Plymouth and Taylor. Street blockage at Dearborn was a source of consternation for the City of Chicago right up to the last days of Dearborn.

The contrasts visible under Dearborn's wooden train-shed and truss-supported platform canopies were amplified inside the station building, which underwent a cosmetic interior modernization following World War II. What even then Chicago's oldest rail terminal was subjected to the well-intentioned indignities of drop ceilings, polished sheet-marble walls and entrances, sliding glass train gates, and fluorescent lighting. The retrofit reflected the Moderne styling tastes prevalent at the time and lent the terminal's interior an upmarket air befitting the Hollywood celebrities who frequented the Santa Fe's resident streamliners.

Mergers lent new names and colors to some Dearborn residents in the terminal's twilight years. Erie became part of Erie Lackawanna in 1960, forsaking two-tone green for gray and maroon in the bargain. Wabash disappeared into Norfolk & Western in 1964, and C&EI's operations into Dearborn were assumed by Louisville & Nashville in 1969 after a brief flirt with Missouri Pacific.

The arrival of Amtrak proved the death knell for Dearborn, despite political forces that had been at work for years to close the station—along with others south of the Loop—and free the railroad land for redevelopment. The campaign, championed by then-Mayor Richard J. Daley, came to naught until the Amtrak era. The Santa Fe duly considered Daley's overture and evaluated an eleventh-hour move to Central Station, but was unable to extricate itself from the terms of its Dearborn lease. A few years before, Santa Fe and Grand Trunk Western had considered the possibility of deserting Dearborn for a new structure, but nothing had come of that idea, either. As events unfolded over the first weekend of May 1971, it was a pair of Santa Fe trains, the *San Francisco Chief* and *Grand Canyon*, that closed Dearborn forever with their arrival on the evening of May 2. The final departure from Dearborn had taken place on April 30 when GTW train

tracks with the more mundane but no less colorful offerings of the Erie, Chicago & Eastern Illinois, Monon, and Wabash. The Grand Trunk Western, a subsidiary of Canadian National Railways, introduced a foreign flair unique among Chicago's terminals, while landlord Chicago & Western Indiana (C&WI) added its diminutive commuter trains to Dearborn's eclectic mix.

The C&WI was, in fact, owned equally by five of the six railroads entering Dearborn. Santa Fe was the odd one out, merely a tenant in the station under the terms of a 999-year lease executed in 1888, and even handling its own terminal switching duties. Trains of the quintet of C&WI owners were switched, appropriately, by C&WI locomotives. To meet its own needs, in 1956 the Santa Fe took the unusual step of having what amounted to a new locomotive model created expressly to switch its trains at Dearborn. Ever-obliging locomotive builder Fairbanks-Morse added a road-switcher-style short hood and installed

156, the vestigial *International Limited*, headed for Port Huron, Michigan.

The N&W's former Wabash commuter operation to Orland Park persisted after Dearborn's closure. The orphaned train terminated on a track adjacent to the venerable terminal, and eventually a small makeshift structure known as Polk Street Station was built at the end of this track to serve the train until it was moved to Union Station in December 1976 under the auspices of the city's Regional Transportation Authority. Trackage south of Dearborn Station was subsequently removed to make way for the Dearborn Park residential community, while the head house survived to house offices, shops, and restaurants as an isolated reminder of Chicago's rich railroad heritage.

CENTRAL STATION

Bearing the baronial hallmarks of contemporary Richardsonian Romanesque design, this lakefront terminal opened on April 7, 1893, just in time to serve the crowds taking in the nearby Columbian Exposition. Ironically, the Exposition showcased the City Beautiful esthetics and Beaux Arts architecture—espoused by Chicago's own Daniel Burnham—that would, in short order, quell the public's taste for the Romanesque trappings of public buildings like Central Station and nearby Dearborn.

Occasionally called 12th Street Station, Central was the southernmost and easternmost of Chicago's major terminals, although it became somewhat more "central" as the city's near-south-side lakefront was filled in after 1915—another legacy of the Columbian Exposition as land was created for Grant Park, the Field Museum, Soldier Field, and other expressions of Burnham's never-fully-realized Chicago Plan. A mile north of Central Station at Michigan Avenue and Randolph Street, the joint IC commuter and Chicago South Shore & South Bend interurban terminal, on the other hand, was (and is) decidedly central. Randolph Street station is easily the rail terminal most convenient to the heart of the Loop shopping district at State and Randolph, two blocks away.

IC's new intercity terminal and headquarters at Michigan Avenue and 12th Street (Roosevelt Road) were designed by Bradford Gilbert and incorporated a six-track trainshed to serve IC mainline trains destined south to New Orleans and intermediate points and, via a portion of the St. Charles Air Line, to northern Illinois and central Iowa. Interestingly, Central was a through-track station although all intercity trains originated and terminated there. (It was physically possible for a train to pass through the station and wind up at stub-end Randolph Street terminal a mile north.) Trains were stored, cleaned, and stocked at IC's Weldon Coach Yard just south of the station, while passenger locomotives were serviced a half mile south at the road's 18th Street Engine Terminal.

RIGHT: Illinois Central's combined station and office building at Michigan and Roosevelt Road as it appeared before an annex was built prior to World War II. The main entrance side of the building—that with the archway—faces north. The carriages and such are on what is in essence the easternmost end of Roosevelt Road/12th Street.—MIKE SCHAFER COLLECTION

BELOW: Stained glass details were a staple in Richardsonian Romanesque architecture. This example was photographed on Central Station's final day of operation on March 5, 1972.
—MIKE SCHAFER

ABOVE: Central Station is in its final day of regular service, March 5, 1972, in this view that looks due north. At lower right, Amtrak's *Panama Limited* is about to enter the train shed as it arrives from New Orleans. Immediately left of the main depot building is the Annex, which supported a huge neon Illinois Central emblem that reverently faced downtown Chicago. IC's electrified suburban tracks bypassed the station at right. Almost the entire area encompassed by this photo was once under water. When IC first built into the city here, it did so on trestlework.—MIKE SCHAFER

RIGHT: Not all boarding or detraining was handled under the train sheds if consists were particularly long. In this 1967 view looking southeast, the rear ends of the southbound *Panama Limited* (at right) and *Seminole* are hanging out north of the depot.—ALAN BRADLEY

The depot's interior layout earned the ire of critics—among them pre-eminent Chicago architect Louis Sullivan—and travelers alike. The waiting room and ticketing area were above both street and track level, forcing passengers to navigate long staircases going up to the waiting room and then down to the platforms—and vice versa.

IC's electrified suburban services did not serve Central directly, instead sharing an adjacent dedicated commuter station (Roosevelt Road) with the orange-and-maroon interurban cars of the South Shore Line.

Central's proximity to the grand public structures on the newly reclaimed lakefront led IC to consider a correspondingly upscale replacement station in the 1920s, at least one architectural rendering of which showed a Beaux Arts structure, but nothing ever came of the notion. A ten-story office annex was added shortly before World War II, with architectural pains taken to emulate the original station's Romanesque detailing despite the annex's boxy, neon-sign-topped form. In common with Dearborn and other classic terminals, Central was subjected to a postwar interior modernization that introduced a drop ceiling and

other "improvements" to Gilbert's arched waiting room. Outside, the station's original clerestory-topped peaked train shed was replaced with a much more sterile low-profile canopy in 1945, utilizing the some of the structural components of the original shed, however.

Under the terms of a 99-year lease, trains of New York Central subsidiaries Michigan Central and Big Four also used Central as their Chicago terminal, though the MC runs were shifted to La Salle Street late in the 1950s. Reportedly these lease agreements—based on earlier lease contracts established by one-time IC lawyer Abraham Lincoln—were so tightly written that New York Central and its successors were not allowed to completely vacate Central Station as long as it was an active station facility. Chesapeake & Ohio trains from Cincinnati also called at Central until their runs were truncated to Hammond, Indiana, during the Depression. Between 1899 and 1914, and again from 1963 to 1965, Central also served as the Wisconsin Central's (later Soo Line) Chicago passenger terminal. Penn Central (PC) became a tenant as a result of the 1968 NYC-Pennsylvania Railroad merger.

Amtrak's southbound *City of New Orleans* (right) and *South Wind* stand ready at Central Station for their 8:30 and 8:40 a.m. respective departures. The famous IC neon sign stands prominent, facing north, atop the Annex; the neon Pepsi sign at left hints at Illinois Central Industries' one-time involvement with Pepsi-Cola.—JIM BOYD

Central Station survived beyond Amtrak's arrival as an intercity passenger terminal, serving Amtrak's Chicago–Champaign–Carbondale, Chicago–New Orleans, Chicago–Florida, and Chicago–Cincinnati–East Coast trains. Central hosted its last scheduled trains on a frigid March 5, 1972 (a steam-powered excursion train would terminate there in 1973), and the next day Amtrak's *Shawnee*, *Panama Limited*, *James Whitcomb Riley*, *George Washington*, and *Floridian* moved across town to Union Station. Central Station was razed in 1974. Today, the site is an upscale condominium/townhouse community known as . . . Central Station Square.

GRAND CENTRAL STATION

Designed by Solon Spencer Beman (1853–1914), a favored architect of the Pullman Company and co-designer of the Pullman planned community on Chicago's South Side, Chicago's Grand Central Station opened on December 8, 1890. The facility traced its origins to the Wisconsin Central Railroad's desire for access to downtown Chicago, in pragmatic partnership with the Chicago, St. Paul & Kansas City, a predecessor to the latter-day Chicago Great Western. Spurned by the Chicago & Western Indiana from access to Dearborn Station, the two roads settled upon a site for their own terminal at what had been a coal yard at Wells and Harrison streets.

In 1888, the WC's plans for Chicago access drew the attention of the Northern Pacific Railroad, itself in search of a direct entry to the city. After a tumultuous period during which the NP leased the WC, reorganized the latter's Chicago properties into a terminal company (the Chicago & Northern Pacific), and then encountered financial difficulties that resulted in the NP defaulting on its lease obligations (causing the WC to lose control of its Chicago assets—the new Grand Central among them), the terminal emerged under the control of the Baltimore & Ohio Railroad. B&O, already a Grand Central tenant, had entered the picture following the reorganization of the Chicago & Northern Pacific, which became the Baltimore & Ohio Chicago Terminal Railroad in 1910.

The "other" Grand Central—Chicago's Grand Central—as it appeared in the summer of 1969 just a few months before its closing. The view looks southeast in early evening. The sign was completely lit up at night, with "Baltimore & Ohio Railroad" appearing in blue neon.—JIM HEUER

ABOVE: **A staircase in the office section of the depot featured wood and wrought-iron trim.**—JIM HEUER

RIGHT: **Grand Central's columned waiting room, complete with fireplace, spoke of quiet grandeur.**—JIM HEUER

Echoing the favored architectural style of its era, Beman's Grand Central was a 471 x 225-foot L-shaped Romanesque mass, punctuated with a 247-foot corner clock tower and sheltering an arched, steel-framed, 119-foot wide x 555-foot-long six-track (stub end) balloon train shed. The brick head house, built on a base of Connecticut brownstone, was embellished with restrained detailing that included carved floral stonework, stained glass, and delicate wrought iron. The same decorative touches were to be found inside the station as well, where arched stained-glass windows marked access to the 70 x 200-foot columned waiting room and substantial wrought-iron gates led to the platforms.

At the time of Grand Central's opening, the only trains served were those of WC, which is why at the time the depot was often referred to as the Wisconsin Central Station. Just under a year later, on December 1, 1891, the B&O became a tenant after shifting its trains from Illinois Central's soon-to-be-replaced lakefront station in favor of Grand Central's relative proximity to the Loop. Chicago Great Western passenger trains used Grand Central after they reached Chicago in 1892, and Pere Marquette trains to and from Michigan called Grand Central home after 1903. WC, for its part, vacated what had been its grand Chicago terminal in 1899. Until it returned to Grand Central in 1914, WC trains relied on IC's Central Station as their Chicago terminal.

With the possible exception of owner B&O and its Chicago–East Coast dual flagships, the *Capitol Limited* and *Columbian*, the occupants of Grand Central could reasonably be characterized, as a group, as the "also-rans" of Chicago's passenger-carrying railroads. No other station in the city had so consistent a cast of marginal (though interesting in their own right) passenger operators, and this was reflected in Grand Central's fortunes as passenger trains on the whole declined after World War II. The Great Western ran its last Chicago passenger train in 1956; the Soo Line abandoned Grand Central—for the second time—in 1963, moving its Chicago–Superior, Wisconsin, *Laker* to Central Station.

Operationally, Grand Central in one aspect stood apart from all other Chicago terminals of the pre-Amtrak

At 3:38 p.m., the south clock on the tower of Grand Central Station appears to be ever so slightly behind, for the Washington-bound *Capitol Limited*, due to depart Chicago's changing skyline at 3:40 P.M., is clearly on its way out of the depot. Time has about run out for Grand Central itself, and later in the fall of 1969 the Solon Spencer Beman-inspired facility will be closed and its steel-wheeled inhabitants moved several blocks north and west to North Western Terminal.—JIM BOYD

Wrought-iron fencing and train gates surrounded the track platforms under Grand Central Station's balloon shed. On this late afternoon circa 1968, the equipment for Chesapeake & Ohio's *Pere Marquette* has been set on track 6 for boarding, and station personnel soon will be rolling back the gate to let Michigan-bound travelers board the Grand Rapids streamliner.—JIM HEUER

era in that arriving trains routinely backed in to the depot. The wye track at which the change in train direction was accomplished was some four miles out of the station, but trains made the back-up move just about as quickly as those few trains that did head straight in.

The last train departed Grand Central on November 8, 1969. The following day, the now-amalgamated C&O/B&O shifted its remaining three daily trains to the awkward but accommodating choice of C&NW's North Western Terminal, and Grand Central was closed.

Cries for its preservation notwithstanding, Grand Central succumbed in 1971, and in its place today stands a bizarre-looking condominium/retail complex. Grand Central lingers in memory as the most-lamented of Chicago's vanished terminals—a diamond in the rough, unappreciated but by a few until it was too late.

LA SALLE STREET STATION

From the din of its namesake thoroughfare, La Salle Street Station was easily mistaken as being just another of Chicago's early twentieth century office towers. In many respects, this is exactly what it was, accommodating the

La Salle Street Station was Chicago's least pretentious major railroad terminal. Hemmed in by the Loop 'L' structure and surrounding buildings, La Salle's facade could not be fully appreciated by pedestrians and passengers arriving to catch trains.—KEVIN HOLLAND COLLECTION

RIGHT: After purchasing transportation at La Salle Street Station's ticketing area on the ground-level floor, passengers proceeded to the second-floor waiting room and concourse via stairs or escalators. The waiting room, shown in 1981 on the last day before the station was closed to make way for a new office building, featured vaulted ceilings.—MARK LLANUZA

BELOW: La Salle Street Station's most esteemed inhabitant was New York Central's *20th Century Limited*, shown having just arrived from New York City in 1963. Rock Island, NYC, and Nickel Plate frequently staged publicity photos at this end of the station, which often lead to the mistaken conclusion that Holabird & Root's 1930 Board of Trade Building looming in the background was part of the terminal.—ALAN BRADLEY

functions of a railroad terminal in the lowermost of its eleven floors. For its relative anonymity in the streetscape, however, La Salle Street Station was notable as the only one of Chicago's six steam railroad terminals providing commuters and long-distance passengers alike with direct access to the elevated ('L') trains of the Loop, Chicago's central business district.

Designed by the Chicago architectural partnership of Frost and Granger, La Salle was opened on July 1, 1903, by the Lake Shore & Michigan Southern Railroad—later an integral part of the New York Central System—and the Chicago, Rock Island & Pacific. The New York, Chicago & St. Louis ("Nickel Plate Road") also used La Salle, but its modest offerings paled against Rock Island's flashy *Rocket*s and *Golden State* and the aristocratic parade of NYC's Great Steel Fleet and its flagship, the *20th Century Limited*. NKP's 1964 successor Norfolk & Western vacated La Salle upon the discontinuance of the last ex-Nickel Plate schedules in September 1965.

continued on page 82

The Nickel Plate Road was very much the "junior partner" at La Salle Street, operating just six daily trains—three in each direction between Chicago and Buffalo—at the peak of the postwar era. In this 1950 view, the consist of NKP train 6 waits beyond the gate, with the indicator's lightning-striped design a reminder of the station's pecking order.—JAY WILLIAMS COLLECTION

79

In the Shadow of Chicago: Joliet Union Station

Of the several busy railroad junctions created in Chicago's orbit as main lines converged on the Windy City, one in particular warranted its own substantial union station. Joliet, Illinois, lies approximately 40 miles southwest of Chicago and was a thriving transportation crossroads in its own right by the late nineteenth century. Eight railroads served Joliet at the turn of the twentieth century, in addition to marine traffic on the newly opened Chicago Sanitary & Ship Canal, which in 1910 replaced an earlier waterway dating to 1848.

The oft-cited demons of downtown congestion and passenger inconvenience were clearly at work in Joliet as the new century entered its second decade, and in 1911 the city's three busiest passenger railroads—the Santa Fe, Rock Island, and the Chicago & Alton (C&A)—jointly formed the Joliet Union Depot Company for the purpose of establishing and operating a union station. Architect Jarvis Hunt was selected to design the facility, which incorporated new elevated approach trackage in addition to the head house itself. These grade-separation efforts had begun in 1908 at the urging of the city, but at that time did not include plans for a consolidated station. The railroads themselves had subsequently proposed the idea of the new passenger facility, and by the end of 1912 it was open and in full operation at the crossing of the Rock Island and C&A/Santa Fe main lines. Michigan Central moved in as a tenant, offering modest service at this, the terminus of its branch from Gary, Indiana.

Joliet Union Station's location adjacent to an elevated 16-diamond mainline crossing called for elaborate signal protection, which was controlled (along with station train movements) by UD Tower, an interlocking plant owned by the Rock Island. While through trains of its three owners were Joliet's mainstay, the Michigan Central, Rock Island, and C&A all originated and terminated schedules at the station as well, and Rock Island fielded a coach yard immediately west of the depot. The elevated tracks called for a two-level station layout, with passengers entering, exiting, and purchasing tickets at street level. A flight of stairs led up to track level and the main waiting room.

Some of the nation's most celebrated passengers literally crossed paths at Joliet. Santa Fe's Chief, Super Chief, El Capitan, and other Chicago–California streamliners were the stainless-steel rivals of the Rock Island's various Rockets, the most far-flung being the Rocky Mountain Rocket. The first streamlined train to serve Joliet, somewhat surprisingly, was operated by the Alton Railroad (the Baltimore & Ohio-owned 1931 successor to the C&A). When the Alton's Abraham Lincoln debuted between Chicago and St. Louis in May 1935, it ushered in a most colorful period in the history of Joliet Union Station. The equipment previously had been operated by the B&O as one of two Royal Blue consists between Washington, D.C., and Jersey City and it was joined on the Alton by the second ex-B&O trainset in 1937, operating between Chicago and St. Louis as the Ann Rutledge. This original equipment could be seen passing through Joliet as late as 1968.

Joliet Union Station's owner list changed again in 1947 when the Alton became part of the Gulf, Mobile & Ohio. During the 1950s, as many as 20 Rock Island, 18 Santa Fe, and 15 GM&O intercity trains called at Joliet Union Station each day, in addition to dozens of commuter runs all but two

UNION STATION, JOLIET, ILL.

Joliet Union Station in its youth in a view that looks southeast. The platform canopy partially visible at track level on the left served the Santa Fe tracks. The thoroughfare on which the auto and horse-and-buggies are standing would later, for a time, be one of famed U.S. Route 66's varied paths through the city. Other than the elimination of the ornate light standards and platform canopies, much of this scene remains unchanged today.—MIKE SCHAFER COLLECTION

belonging to Rock Island (GM&O ran one commuter each way on weekdays). Even with the coming of Amtrak in May 1971, Joliet remained a "union" station. The Rock Island continued to operate its own—by then admittedly modest—intercity schedules until 1979, serving the Quad Cities and Peoria from Chicago's La Salle Street Station. The remnants of Santa Fe and GM&O intercity service through Joliet, on the other hand, were operated by Amtrak.

After the Rock Island was liquidated in 1980, the Chicago & North Western—backed by Chicago's Regional Transportation Authority (RTA)—briefly stepped in to maintain the former-CR&IP commuter services to Joliet. The RTA subsequently became the oversight body for the new (mid-1980s) Northeast Illinois Regional Commuter Rail Corporation—better known as Metra—which assumed responsibility for operation of the remaining ex-GM&O commuter service (GM&O having merged with Illinois Central in 1972 to form Illinois Central Gulf).

Joliet Union Station remained in the hands of its railroad owners after Amtrak's creation—Santa Fe and Illinois Central Gulf with one-third each, and Metra inheriting the Rock Island's portion. On April 20, 1987, the Santa Fe and ICG shares were bought by the City of Joliet as a prelude to renovation of the facility, with Metra retaining its one-third share. Long-overdue structural repairs were made, and vestiges of the terminal's declining years—the waiting room's false ceiling chief among them—were removed. The original waiting room, while restored, was curiously closed off to traffic in anticipation of reuse for other purposes. Interior marble and tile benefited from a thorough cleaning, as did the station's Beaux-Arts limestone exterior. Improvements also extended to platforms, lighting, signage, and even new commuter train layover facilities at the rebuilt ex-Michigan Central yard east of the station.

Of all the railroad terminals in "Chicagoland," Joliet Union Station—from an outward appearance at least—remains the most unchanged. About the only major missing components are the platform canopies, removed many decades ago. Aside from being an anchor to Joliet's re-emerging downtown, JUS is also a popular train-watching location, not only for students of railroading, but for local families as well who wish to show their children that railroading still exudes an aura of excitement.

Its locomotive straddling the intersection with the Santa Fe and Gulf, Mobile & Ohio main lines, Rock Island's Chicago-bound *Peoria Rocket* pauses at Joliet Union Station in the spring of 1965. A portion of Rock Island's suburban train layover tracks is visible at left.—MIKE SCHAFER

Historically, La Salle Street Station had been dominated by the Chicago, Rock Island & Pacific which, in addition to a fleet of intercity passenger trains, fielded a comprehensive suburban train service to Blue Island (on two different routes) and Joliet. New York Central commuter service into La Salle Street was limited at best, lasting into the early 1960s, and the Nickel Plate Road did not offer true commuter service. In this view from the Roosevelt Road overpass on April 30, 1971, a Joliet-bound "Rock" suburban train leaves behind a La Salle Street Station that will, the following day, be unaffected by the newly created Amtrak.—JIM HEUER

Continued from page 79

In addition to its intercity *Rocket*s, the Rock Island operated a significant commuter service out of La Salle to Blue Island and Joliet. In the station's halcyon postwar days, the Rock Island's commuter business accounted for the lion's share of La Salle's nearly 200 daily trains and 450,000 weekly passengers.

In marked contrast to its impact on Chicago's other terminals, the coming of Amtrak had little effect at La Salle Street. As a condition of the 1968 NYC-PRR merger that created Penn Central, La Salle's remaining ex-NYC services had already been shifted to Union Station. Rock Island, La Salle's lone remaining occupant, opted not to join Amtrak and continued to operate a modest intercity schedule to Peoria, Illinois, and the Quad Cities (Davenport and Bettendorf, Iowa, and Rock Island and Moline, Illinois) until 1979. By that time, the Rock Island's commuter operations had been assumed by the Regional Transportation Authority and would be passed on to Metra in the 1980s.

With its prime location at the edge of the Loop, La Salle Street Station succumbed to real-estate pressures in 1981 and was demolished to make way for new office developments. Metra service over former Rock Island routes was retained at a compact pseudo-Art Deco facility on the redeveloped site.

In mid-2000, plans were under way to move some of Metra's trains from crowded Union Station over to the new La Salle Street Station. In addition, Amtrak and the Illinois Department of Transportation were also mulling the possibility of terminating their planned high-speed Chicago–St. Louis trains at the La Salle site, enabling the new trains to enter Chicago on the former Rock Island alignment from Joliet rather than their current ex-GM&O route.

NORTH WESTERN TERMINAL

Frost and Granger, the architects responsible for La Salle Street Station, designed this massive Renaissance-style terminal for the Chicago & North Western as one of several commissions they undertook for the railroad. The two architects happened to be brothers-in-law, and their body of work for the North Western may have been influenced, at least in part, by the fact that each had become the son-in-law of C&NW President Marvin Hughitt, through marriage to his daughters.

Opened on January 3, 1911, the terminal's 16 platform tracks were reached by six approach tracks and sheltered under an 894-foot-long Bush train shed. North Western Terminal was unique among Chicago's "big six" in that it served as a one-railroad facility for virtually all of its existence, the sole exception being the 18-month interlude during which the remaining intercity schedules of the affiliated Chesapeake & Ohio/Baltimore & Ohio were hosted following the closure of Grand Central Station in 1969.

LEFT: This postcard view looks northeasterly and depicts North Western Terminal shortly after its opening in 1911. Note the low facade extending north along Clinton Street, at left. Ground-level facilities—beneath the elevated tracks—housed a post-office substation, a commuter concourse, baggage and express facilities, and, farther up Clinton Street, the terminal's power plant.—MIKE SCHAFER COLLECTION

BELOW: The main waiting room of North Western Terminal in 1979, looking east. Ticket windows are at right, having been moved to this, the terminal's upper level, from their original ground-level location. The concourse and platform tracks were reached through the colonnade at left.—MIKE MC BRIDE

ABOVE: This rare view of North Western Terminal from the southwest was made possible for a few weeks after buildings on adjacent blocks were torn down and shows the two-story facade along Clinton Street to good advantage.—MARK LLANUZA

RIGHT: By the end of the 1980s, the new skyscrapers populating downtown Chicago included one built on the rubble of the 1911 North Western Terminal head house. In this 1987 view of a C&NW executive special about to depart the Chicago terminal for Bill, Wyoming, the new, glass-sheathed Northwestern Atrium Center dominates the background. The photo includes a close-up of one of the unique "dwarf" signals that controlled movements in and out of the platform tracks. The disc rotated to provide three different signal-light indications (red, yellow, green) along with three positions of the painted-on semaphore bar (horizontal as shown, diagonal, and vertical).—MIKE SCHAFER

84

The day after Grand Central Station closed, C&O/B&O trains—like the *Capitol Limited* shown here on November 9, 1969—began using the C&NW station.—JIM HEUER

Upon passing through the main waiting room and upper-level concourse, passengers found themselves at the south end of North Western Terminal's stub tracks, all under the cover of a massive Bush train shed. Track 15's indicator board was being ministered to in 1984.—MIKE MC BRIDE

The trains of the C&NW's extensive commuter service—with three main routes fanning west, northwest, and north out of downtown Chicago—shared the train shed (but not entirely a concourse) with the railroad's famous *"400"* intercity fleet and, from the 1930s into October 1955, the Overland Route's *Challenger* and *City* trains operated in conjunction with the Union Pacific and Southern Pacific railroads. Commuters, who typically accounted for two-thirds of the station's traffic in the late 1940s and 1950s, had the option of using their own dedicated concourse accessible from street level as well as the main concourse. Intercity passengers used the main concourse exclusively which—along with the station's 102 x 202-foot x 84-foot-high waiting room, restaurant, shops, and track access—was located on the second (track) level. Even the ticket office was later moved upstairs.

Just north of the station at ground level was the Erie Street commuter coach yard where most commuter train sets were stored during day layover between rush hours; intercity passenger trains were serviced at the 40th Street yard several miles west of the station, requiring long back-up equipment moves. Erie Street yard was replaced by a new facility built to service C&NW's new bilevel "Commuter Streamliners" (as the road dubbed its modernized suburban train fleet) that were introduced early in the 1950s. The new facility was (and is) located about two miles west on the West Line at Western Avenue.

North Western Terminal suffered a fate similar to La Salle's and was closed in 1984. The C&NW's imposing Renaissance head house, with its crown jewel vaulted-ceiling waiting room, was then demolished to make way for the Northwestern [sic] Atrium Center, an impressive glass-sheathed Art Deco-styled office tower completed in 1987; it featured a lofty, double-level, escalator-equipped concourse area for commuters not wishing to use the sub-platform concourses. As with La Salle's redevelopment, Metra service was retained and integrated in the new project, with the station area known after 1997 as the Richard B. Ogilvie Transportation Center. Metra undertook a $93-million, four-year rehabilitation that thoroughly renewed the erstwhile terminal's platforms, train shed, trackage, commuter concourse, and mechanical systems in the early 1990s.

-90 Birds' Eye View of New Union Station, Chicago.

ABOVE: Taken from the vantage point of a commercial building with an accommodating tenant, this spring 1969 view recorded the Chicago Union Station complex in its eleventh hour, weeks before demolition commenced on the concourse building closest to the camera. The two tracks adjacent to the Chicago River were the station's only through tracks. All the rest were divided into north and south stub-end groups by the concourse.—JIM BOYD

LEFT: This early 1920s postcard shows an artist's impression of the then-yet-to-be-completed station. The differences are many, from the low-profile concourse building to a head house reminiscent of Jacksonville Terminal. Other contemporary postcards showed the station topped with a soaring 20-story office tower, a feature proposed by the architects and allowed for in the foundation construction, but never executed.—MIKE SCHAFER COLLECTION

CHICAGO UNION STATION

Chicago's youngest terminal was opened on July 23, 1925, by owner railroads Pennsylvania; Chicago, Burlington & Quincy; and Chicago, Milwaukee, St. Paul & Pacific ("The Milwaukee Road") after a protracted dozen-year construction period. Architectural work was undertaken by Graham, Burnham & Co. from 1913 to 1917, and by Graham, Anderson, Probst & White after 1917. The station was situated on the west bank of the Chicago River's South Branch, just two blocks south of North Western Terminal.

Union Station was designed as two structures, connected by an underground passage beneath the roadway (Canal Street) that separated them. Immediately abutting the river was the concourse building, the open interior of which harkened to New York's Pennsylvania Station—not surprising given the PRR's status as Union Station's majority owner. On the west side of Canal Street, the station's colonnade-fronted head house contained the 112-foot-high, skylight-capped main waiting room along with ticketing and baggage-handling facilities. The architects envisioned a 20-story office tower atop the head house, and the station structure employed a foundation suitable for a building of that size, although the office tower as built only reached a height of eight stories.

The notion of Union Station as a divided structure—unintentionally symbolic of the city's "invisible barrier" to through services pilloried by Robert R. Young—was furthered by its track layout, which took the form of two back-to-back stub-ended terminals. Token through trackage (track No. 28 plus a non-platformed track) adjacent to

Chicago Union Station's head house, located on the west side of Canal Street across from the concourse building, housed the terminal's main waiting room. Even in 1969, when this view was recorded, the 112-foot-high hall was a busy—if somewhat gloomy—place. (The gloominess was alleviated in the 1980s when the World War II-era blackout paint was removed from the skylight windows and the hall's interior cleaned by Amtrak.) A passage under Canal Street linked the two parts of the terminal.—JIM HEUER

the river was never employed as such in scheduled pre-Amtrak service, but it was used to accommodate extra-long train consists. The nine stub platform tracks to the north of the station served trains of the Milwaukee Road, foremost of which were the swift *Hiawatha*s. On the south side, 13 stub tracks were devoted to trains of the PRR and Burlington, as well as tenant Chicago & Alton (which merged into Gulf, Mobile & Ohio in 1947). By virtue of the Burlington's pooled West Coast services operated in conjunction with Great Northern and Northern Pacific, trains of the latter two roads also served Union Station.

Division worked in Union's favor when it came to marshalling the flow of passengers, baggage, mail, and express. Platforms were laid out to permit simultaneous loading or unloading of passengers and head-end traffic from opposite sides of the same train, while inside the station these two conflicting traffic flows were handled on separate levels.

Even if La Salle Street Station could lay claim to hosting the "world's most famous train" (in the guise of NYC's *20th Century Limited*), Union Station was hardly outclassed. Over the years, Union hosted such landmark liners as PRR's *Broadway Limited* and *General*, Burlington's haute *Denver Zephyr*, the joint CB&Q-Rio Grande-Western Pacific *California Zephyr*, GN's *Empire Builder*, NP's *North Coast Limited*, and Milwaukee Road's stellar *Olympian Hiawatha*.

When it came to such streamlined novelties as domes and "signature" observation cars, no other Chicago station approached Union for sheer volume and variety. The Burlington had pioneered the introduction of dome cars to revenue service in 1945, and its enthusiasm rubbed off on pool partners GN and NP to the degree that Union was the nation's *de facto* dome capital for a quarter century. For its part, the Milwaukee Road became a dome devotee in 1952 when it introduced full-length "Super Domes" to its *Hiawatha* fleet. The Milwaukee's biggest contribution to Union's appeal, however, lay in the road's affection for unorthodox observation cars, whether in the form of 1930s "Beaver-Tails" or 1940s "Skytops." Chicago's other terminals all had their share of streamlined observation cars, and domes eventually infiltrated all of them as well, but Union cornered the "feature-car" market by any definition.

Union's residents may have weathered the general decline in passenger train fortunes better than their counterparts at Chicago's other stations, but by the time the PRR had become half of troubled Penn Central in 1968, the prospects for any railroad-operated passenger trains in the U.S. were undeniably bleak.

The outlook was equally uncertain for Union Station itself, at a time when the city's other stations had begun to close. In 1969, Union's stately concourse building was razed—ominously recalling the fate six years before of Pennsylvania Station, the New York City landmark which it so resembled. CUS concourse air rights were exploited by the Gateway Center office complex—specifically, by the drab new 222 South Riverside building—and the former concourse's train-service functions were shoehorned into an inadequate subterranean cinder-block annex, still connected via a tunnel to the station's surviving main waiting room and head house.

While Amtrak's 1971 debut meant the demise of intercity services at Chicago's other terminals—whether suddenly, as at Dearborn and North Western, or over a period of months, as was the case at Central—it meant new routes added to Union's historical mix as the nation's new passenger train operator consolidated its Chicago terminal operations. The most convoluted of Union Station's new Amtrak routes were those formerly served by Central Station, which after March 5, 1972, were obliged to reach their new cross-town terminal via the elevated St. Charles Air Line and a time-consuming back-up move.

The prospects of greater stability at Chicago's only active intercity passenger terminal materialized in 1984 when Amtrak took title to the complex from Milwaukee

With morning sun streaming in, passengers queue in Union Station's concourse for a south-side departure on October 11, 1964. When this building was razed in 1969 to accommodate air-rights development, its replacement was a cramped cinder-block bunker, deemed adequate by planners who assumed that Union Station itself would soon follow the concourse building into oblivion. Time proved the planners wrong, and although Amtrak made significant improvements to the concourse in 1991, present-day passengers are still impacted by the shortsightedness of the 1969 demolition.—JOHN GRUBER

Union Station's south arrival tracks hosted a typically colorful trio on the morning of October 11, 1964. The Gulf, Mobile & Ohio's *Midnight Special* is sandwiched between the Burlington's *Black Hawk/Mainstreeter/Western Star* and the Pennsylvania's *Buckeye/Kentuckian.*—JOHN GRUBER

Road and from CB&Q's 1970 successor Burlington Northern (Amtrak had acquired Penn Central's shares of the property in 1977). Among much-needed improvements, the head house was renovated and cleaned, with the waiting room restored to an approximation of its former elegance and brightened by the removal of skylight blackout paint dating to World War II. At about the same time, Amtrak instituted a major operational change when it began backing nearly all arriving long-distance trains (except those that approached from the north) into the station in an effort to reduce locomotive exhaust pollution in the depot area and reduce equipment moves during layover and servicing.

A $32-million, two-year makeover of the cramped concourse area was completed in 1991. Gone was the 1969-vintage cinder-block "warehouse" decor, replaced with a more upscale Art Deco look complete with improved lighting, coffered ceilings, information display, and train gate access. Of particular benefit to Amtrak travelers was a reorientation of commuter pedestrian flow via an enlarged mezzanine area. Assuming that intercity passenger service would soon be vanished, planners responsible for the 1969 layout had never adequately accommodated the needs of intercity passengers in the facility's cramped quarters. Also new in 1991 were a first-class "Metropolitan Lounge" for Amtrak sleeping-car passengers and enlarged north and south concourse waiting areas with a combined 900-seat capacity. The introduction of relocated ticketing and baggage-claim facilities brought all of Amtrak's station functions into the newly remodeled area, supplanting the original headhouse waiting room across Canal Street.

For more than a decade, Amtrak has entertained proposals to develop the head house air rights while preserving the 1925 waiting room's appearance and function. In essence, the original architects' vision of a highrise office tower would be realized, with one proposal calling for the existing eight-story structure's replacement with a pair of 24-story towers. In another proposal that eerily mimics that of New York's Pennsylvania Station, the now-vacated Chicago Post Office building adjacent to Union (and positioned over the south approach tracks) has been eyed as a future new terminal for the emerging Midwest high-speed rail corridor project.

EPILOGUE

Of Chicago's one-time sextet of classic terminal structures, only portions of the oldest and youngest remain. Dearborn's disembodied head house pays silent tribute to a generation of terminals whose architecture fell from fashion, ironically, at the hands of a Chicagoan. Union Station, itself a late example of Daniel Burnham's Beaux-Arts triumph, emerged as the city's sole functioning survivor, still fulfilling the purpose for which it was built as the city grew around and above it.

This 1984 view—recorded after Amtrak had assumed ownership of Chicago Union Station—looks down the northeast stairwell into the restored main waiting room. One of Amtrak's most visible improvements was removal of the blackout coating from the waiting room skylight, enabling sunshine to brighten the vast room for the first time in decades— compare this view to that on page 87. If the hall looks familiar, it may be due to Union Station's sporadic use as a period motion picture and television production set. One scene of the motion picture "The Sting" was filmed near the bottom of these stairs.
—MIKE MC BRIDE

⑤ SOUTHERN DELIGHTS

• RICHMOND • JACKSONVILLE • TAMPA • ATLANTA • LOUISVILLE
• NASHVILLE • CHATTANOOGA • NEW ORLEANS

At the peak of the American passenger train's importance—between, say, the end of World War I and the onset of the Great Depression—the Southeastern U.S. offered as eclectic a range of railroad terminals as could be found in any other region of the country. The Southeast was particularly notable, however, for its terminals built primarily to handle that emerging commodity, the tourist. Quite apart from the regional ebb-and-flow of rail traffic found throughout America, the Southeast early on witnessed a superimposed "overhead" traffic pattern of prosperous vacationers from the likes of Chicago, Detroit, and New York. Ensconced aboard deluxe—and often seasonal—trains like the *Orange Blossom Special* and *Floridan*, these travelers passed through Dixie en route to the newly developed terminals and resorts of Florida and Gulf Coast points in Louisiana and Alabama. Even in the era of lightweight streamlined trains—before the bulk of this tourist traffic literally went overhead—this pattern meant survival for terminals like Jacksonville, Tampa, and New Orleans.

ABOVE: The interior of Nashville Union Station was an artistic feast, replete with bas reliefs and murals such as this of a Ten-Wheeler rushing along with an express train.—JIM HEUER

LEFT: Broad Street Station, Richmond, in December 1973. Not well known, but just visible in this photo, is the following inscription over the main entrance, revealing its intended name: UNION STATION OF RICHMOND. The domed structure's resemblance to the Jefferson Memorial is hardly coincidental. Broad Street Station's architect, John Russell Pope, went on to design that Washington, D.C. landmark, dedicated in 1943—six years after Pope's death—on the bicentennial of Jefferson's birth. Echoes of Jefferson's own architectural tastes can be seen in both structures. Pope's work in the nation's capital also includes the National Archives Building and the National Gallery of Art.
—MIKE SCHAFER

The Florida-bound RF&P-SCL *Everglades*, en route from Washington, D.C., to Jacksonville, was being serviced at Richmond on April 24, 1971—just a week before Amtrak made its debut. Regardless of their actual timetable direction, Broad Street Station's ingenious track layout ensured that all trains passed through in this orientation.—MIKE SCHAFER

RICHMOND UNION STATION

Like so many of its contemporaries, the Union Station of Richmond, Virginia—more popularly known as Broad Street Station—owed its creation, in large measure, to civic and passenger frustration with the status quo. Two of the railroads serving Richmond—the Richmond, Fredericksburg & Potomac and the Richmond & Petersburg (an Atlantic Coast Line predecessor)—opened a joint station in 1887 to replace outmoded facilities and augment the RF&P's existing station at Pine and Broad streets (built in 1880). Civic leaders had been determined to see the railroads' stations and associated trackage removed from the

downtown area to eliminate traffic congestion and pedestrian hazards, and passengers using the new shared station faced less daunting arrangements when making connections between trains.

The grandly named Richmond, Fredericksburg & Potomac & Richmond & Petersburg Connection Railway made it possible for the same trains to serve both stations, but variations on the earlier problems of congestion and passenger dissatisfaction persisted. Finally, in 1913, the two railroads announced plans for the construction of a new joint station northwest of city center, to be built on a former fairground acquired by the RF&P in 1904 and developed by the railroad as the Hermitage Country Club. Following a design competition, architect John Russell Pope (1874-1937) of New York was awarded the commission for the new station. Pope, a disciple of McKim and devout Classicist, subsequently became well known as the architect responsible for the Jefferson Memorial, National Archives, and the National Gallery of Art in Washington, D.C., so the similarities between Broad Street Station and some of those Washington landmarks is not a coincidence.

Construction of Richmond's new station finally commenced in January 1917, after nearly four years of acrimonious debate between the city and the two railroads. During that time, the RF&P and R&P declined the city's suggestion to become tenants in Richmond's new Main Street Station, which served trains of competitors Chesapeake & Ohio and Seaboard Air Line. The RF&P and the R&P held their ground, quite literally, and unveiled plans in the spring of 1916 for their new "Hermitage Station" and its novel track layout.

Rather than being directly on the main artery serving RF&P and ACL through trains, the station was positioned on a loop that comprised the end of a very short branch off the nearby main line. The branch was linked to the main line via wye tracks, so that either north- or southbound trains entered the branch, the loop, and the station facing the same way (southeast). Upon departure, trains completed the rest of their brief journey through the loop and returned to the mainline junction, where they could turn either north or south. This ingenious trackage arrangement, which also allowed all locomotive-servicing facilities to be at one end of the station, was the work of civil engineer Harold Frazier.

Following delays and cost overruns precipitated by the United States' involvement in World War I, the Union Station opened to traffic on January 6, 1919, at a cost of almost $3 million. Its Broad Street address proved sufficiently memorable that the facility quickly came to be known simply, and lastingly, as Broad Street Station.

The station's design was reflective of the Beaux-Arts movement prevalent in the first decades of the twentieth century, and is notable for its dome—a favored element of Pope's. The colonnade, rotunda, and dome—inspired by the Pantheon—were hallmarks of what came to be regarded as the most attractive railroad terminal in Virginia.

Broad Street echoed the traffic pattern experienced by so many of the classic terminals, achieving its peak during

Beyond the polished wooden benches within the station's rotunda, a columned portal led to the concourse area over the tracks. Within a few months of this spring 1975 view, Amtrak would vacate Broad Street for a brand-new facility.—MIKE SCHAFER

Jacksonville Terminal remained a busy place in 1968, due in no small measure to the number of vacationers still opting to travel from the Northeast to Florida by rail instead of air. Though home to such celebrity trains as the *Silver Meteor* and *Champion*, Jacksonville Terminal was also still being called upon by several workaday trains such as this *Gulf Coast Special* just in from New York. —JIM BOYD

World War II when almost 60 daily trains were handled; approximately ten million passengers passed through during 1943.

Its location between Washington and the resorts of the Southeast and Florida made Broad Street an especially colorful—and busy—spot in the postwar era. The RF&P handled the ACL's sun-bound streamliners to and from Washington Union Station, with ACL taking over south of Richmond. Coast Line's postwar parade included the famous *Champion* streamliners as well as the *Florida Special, Palmetto, Everglades*, and the *Vacationer*.

Even with the relatively strong Florida traffic that passed through Richmond well into the 1960s, Broad Street was not immune from the nationwide postwar decline in rail travel. In 1958, as DC-8s and 707s were poised to pluck stalwart sunseekers from the rails, the

wryly named Seaboard Air Line Railroad vacated Main Street Station on the southeast side of downtown and moved its remaining schedules into Broad Street—not an easy task. Because of the way in which SAL trackage was linked to the RF&P main line, northbound Seaboard trains had to back into Broad Street and southbounds had to back out after their stop.

The Seaboard Coast Line merger of July 1967 combined ACL and SAL, and reverted Broad Street to a two-railroad terminal. Amtrak arrived on May 1, 1971, and held on at Broad Street until November 15, 1975. By this time, the loop track had been severed, and all Amtrak trains had to back into the terminal. The State of Virginia purchased the property the following year. Initial plans to raze the station and develop the site as a state office park thankfully never came to fruition. In January 1976, the

In a ritual almost as old as passenger trains themselves, travelers check in for their train under the requisite signs for coach and sleeping-car space. In this instance, Seaboard Coast Line's northbound *Champion* is being loaded at Jacksonville Terminal on February 6, 1970.—JIM NEUBAUER

Jacksonville Terminal Company
UNION STATION

O. B. Acker, Ticket Agent

PHONES:
Information, 5-3801
Ticket Office, 5-0259

Railroad fare $............ } Includes 15% Tax
Pullman fare ....
Insurance $............
TOTAL $............

Car............

Space............

Train............

Your train departs at............M.

When they purchased passage at one of Jacksonville Terminal's ticket windows, passengers received their tickets in an envelope like this.
—KEVIN J. HOLLAND COLLECTION

hitherto homeless Science Museum of Virginia secured permission from the State to occupy a portion of the station for temporary exhibits. The museum never left.

On January 6, 1977—the 58th anniversary of Broad Street Station's opening—Governor Godwin officially rededicated the facility as the permanent home of the Science Museum of Virginia. Pope's magnificent station survives as the heart of an interactive educational facility incorporating, among many features, a planetarium and Imax™ theater. Over a quarter-century after the last passenger train departed, traces of the station's railroad heritage remain: Three platform tracks were reinstalled to accommodate displayed railroad equipment. The complex also houses a model railroad club.

FLORIDA

Jacksonville Terminal

In its role as the *de facto* rail passenger gateway to Florida, Jacksonville Terminal was the largest station—with the most daily train movements and heaviest passenger volume—south of Washington, D.C.. From its opening on November 18, 1919, the $3.5-million terminal served as a conduit through which Northeastern and Midwestern vacationers passed to and from their seasonal Florida sojourns. Reflecting this traffic pattern, a remarkable 85 percent of Jacksonville Terminal's arriving passengers carried on to other destinations, with only a change of trains, the switching of through cars, or perhaps a brief stroll along the platform the only manifestation of their visit to Jacksonville.

Jacksonville Terminal was built by the group of railroads that were also its owners, under the auspices of their jointly held Jacksonville Terminal Company. The Seaboard Air Line, Atlantic Coast Line, and Florida East Coast each owned 25 percent of the Terminal Company's stock; the Southern Railway and its Georgia, Southern & Florida subsidiary split the remaining quarter-interest 50/50.

In 1904—only 14 years after the first passenger train traveled south across Jacksonville's St. Johns River—the

continued on page 100

This painting by Mark Harland Johnson presents one of Jacksonville Terminal's more colorful postwar denizens—and that in a station with no shortage of rainbow-hued trains. The *Champion* was an all-coach streamlined train that entered service between New York's Pennsylvania Station and Miami on December 1, 1939. In the course of its run, the *Champion* operated over the rails of the PRR, RF&P, ACL, and FEC. Of the three Budd-built stainless-steel consists needed to protect the schedule, two were owned by the Atlantic Coast Line. The third was owned by Florida East Coast, and is depicted here being led out of Jacksonville Terminal by FEC E3A No. 1002. The nearby bridge across the St. Johns River marked the FEC's sole point of connection with the "outside world."—MARK HARLAND JOHNSON

UNION STATION, TAMPA, FLA.

This early postcard gives a glimpse of Tampa Union Station's unassuming street side.—JOE WELSH COLLECTION

Left to right, the Tampa/St. Petersburg sections of the *Silver Meteor*, *City of Miami*, and the *Champion*—all northbound—at Tampa Union Station early in 1968.—JIM BOYD

Continued from page 97

Terminal Company opened its first Union Station on a site near the waterway. With railroads fueling the growth of Florida's seaside resorts in a symbiotic frenzy, the mission-style structure soon proved inadequate to handle the lucrative traffic which its owners were helping to create. A replacement was needed, and architect Murchison K. Mackenzie of New York produced the winning entry in a Terminal Company design competition. Mackenzie created a columned 360 x 78-foot Beaux Arts terminal building which accommodated 14 stub-end tracks and 11 through

tracks. The 1904 station survived and was incorporated into the new Terminal complex as a baggage facility. An 11-stall roundhouse and a 115-car coach yard provided servicing for equipment.

The seasonal nature of its traffic dictated that JT be large enough to accommodate a winter rush of as many as 115 trains and over 20,000 passengers each day. Terminal employment could almost double during the peak season, from a typical 1,200-person summer roster to as many as 2,000 in the Terminal's halcyon winters.

The station's stub tracks served originating and terminating schedules. This was where the Southern's trains were to be found, along with SAL's New Orleans through services. Through trains to south Florida, logically, employed the station's through tracks and accessed FEC rails via a large bascule bridge just east of the Terminal (this was the FEC's only connection to the rest of the nation's rail network). Depending upon their point of origin and destination, however, certain through trains arrived at and departed from JT by backing into the station, effectively using a through track as a stub. Trains in this category included those to Florida's west coast, as well as SAL's south Florida schedules after they gave up FEC tracks for SAL's own newly opened Miami route in 1927. This led to the incongruity of rival ACL and SAL trains, both destined for Miami but seemingly headed in opposite directions within the confines of the Terminal.

Jacksonville Terminal employed a fleet of 0-6-0 steam and alligator-bedecked Electro-Motive (a General Motors subsidiary) diesel locomotives to handle as many as 500

daily switching operations during peak season. Many of these moves involved coaches and Pullman sleeping cars, both occupied and empty. JT's switchers also handled up to 300 daily express, baggage, and mail cars during peak periods, with most of the express business involving north-bound shipments of grapefruit, oranges, fish, and other perishable products.

While railroad travel across the U.S. was quick to feel the impact of airline growth, passenger trains to and from Florida were particularly hard hit. Eastern Airlines made history when it introduced jet service on the lucrative New York-Miami route in December 1958—the first domestic passenger jet operation in America. As World War II ended, Jacksonville Terminal handled an average of 105 trains per day. In 1972—Amtrak's first full year of operation—barely a dozen trains called at JT, on average, each day.

After strike-related sabotage obliged FEC to withdraw from the operation of relaying through trains to and from southern Florida points in 1963, passenger trains traveling south of JT were faced with a lengthy reverse movement to reach the Terminal. On January 3, 1974, Jacksonville Terminal served its last passenger train—Amtrak's *Floridian*. The next day, Amtrak trains began using a far more modest facility erected on the outskirts of Jacksonville, adjacent to what had by then become the Seaboard Coast Line main line. The inefficient back-up move was history—and so, it seemed, was Jacksonville Terminal. After proposals to convert the station into a restaurant and hotel complex came to naught, the Terminal's tracks were lifted in 1977. Public awareness of the structure and the desire for its preservation remained high enough that 8,000 persons paid $10 each to attend a November 1977 waiting room gala sponsored by Riverside Avondale Preservation. Salvation for Jacksonville Terminal finally came in 1992, when it was reopened following rehabilitation as part of the Prime Osborn III Convention Center. The 1974 station on the city's western fringe, meanwhile, remains ample for Amtrak's needs.

TAMPA UNION STATION

Tampa Union Station was opened in 1912 as a joint venture of the Atlantic Coast Line, the Seaboard Air Line, and the Tampa Northern railroads and consolidated the city's previously independent stations. The station's column-facade, compact, rectangular head house abutted stub-end platform tracks, though a through-track platform to one side of the station served trains that operated through to and from Clearwater and St. Petersburg.

Tampa was an important connecting point between the Tampa/St. Petersburg sections of mainline trains from the Northeast and Midwest and various secondary runs to places like Naples and Boca Raton, so train time yielded a fascinating array of station movements. Trains would be

6A-H2583

backing in and out of the depot while the station switcher busily transferred through cars from one train consist to another. When Amtrak arrived in May 1971, much of this activity was curtailed, and eventually Amtrak pulled out of St. Petersburg, terminating all its west coast Florida runs at Tampa Union.

The deteriorating structure was closed in 1984, and Amtrak's administrative functions were relocated to an adjacent trailer. An organization known as Tampa Union Station Preservation and Redevelopment, Inc. was established at that time to ensure that all possible adaptive reuse options were considered. The group purchased the terminal from CSX Transportation (corporate successor to the station's original owners) in 1991. Twelve thousand supporters were on hand on May 7, 1998, as Tampa Union Station was officially reopened after a $2.6-million restoration. After a 13-year hiatus the terminal once again hosted Amtrak trains, and over 54,000 Amtrak passengers used the facility in 1999.

ATLANTA, GEORGIA

Terminal Station

Atlanta's Terminal Station traced its origins to the February 10, 1903, creation of the Atlanta Joint Terminal Company by the Central of Georgia, Southern, and Atlanta & West Point railroads. Two years later, on May 3, 1905, Terminal Station opened at the corner of Mitchell Street and Madison Avenue. Washington architect P. Thornton Mayre envisioned his Renaissance-revival head house, with its elaborate towers and arched facade, as a grand "gateway to the South."

A "Gateway to the South," Atlanta's Terminal Station opened in 1905. The statue in the foreground of this 1930s postcard view was that of Samuel Spencer, first president of the Southern Railway. When Terminal Station closed in 1970, the railway relocated Spencer's statue to Peachtree Station, where it could preside over Southern's remaining passenger trains.

—KEVIN J. HOLLAND COLLECTION

RIGHT: Terminal Station's overhead concourse, visible above the head-end cars in this 1967 track-level view of SCL's *Silver Comet,* actually extended from the rear of the head house at its ground-floor level.—A.M. LANGLEY, JR.

BELOW: A June 1957 Terminal Station scene illustrates how the tracks were placed below street level. The matched WofA and A&WP FP7s handled the *Crescent Limited* on its leg west of Atlanta to Montgomery, where L&N took over for the rest of the run to New Orleans. Note how the station's twin towers have been truncated, in comparison with the postcard view on the previous page.—HOWARD ROBINS

Mayre's twin-towered, red-tile-roofed head house overlooked the station's platform tracks, which were reached by passengers via an overhead concourse. When it opened, Terminal Station hosted trains of its three owners along with those of the Atlanta, Birmingham & Atlantic (later Atlanta, Birmingham & Coast, then ACL) and Seaboard Air Line railroads. During the 1930s almost 80 trains a day called at Terminal Station. Because of the alignment of the SAL and Southern Railway main lines through Atlanta, competing through trains of both lines between Birmingham and Washington, D.C., had to endure lengthy detours to enter Terminal Station, with the SAL's trains opting for an awkward back-up move.

By 1968, the first full year after ACL and SAL had merged to form Seaboard Coast Line, 26 trains a day were still using Terminal Station, versus just ten at nearby Union Station.

Terminal Station was closed in June 1970 after the Southern Railway discontinued several trains and shifted two of its three survivors—the new *Southern Crescent* and the *Piedmont*—to suburban Peachtree Station. Meanwhile, the Atlanta–Savannah *Nancy Hanks* of SR subsidiary

Central of Georgia was moved to a small depot on Spring Street. Atlanta's venerable Terminal Station was demolished in 1971.

Union Station

Of Atlanta's two main twentieth century railroad terminals, Union Station was the younger and also the smaller. Opened on April 18, 1930, Union Station was just three blocks from its middle-aged neighbor, Terminal Station. The newer station served trains of Atlantic Coast Line, Louisville & Nashville, and the Georgia Railroad. Like Terminal, Union Station had through tracks, and the approach tracks of both were linked. Union Station survived to Amtrak's startup on May 1, 1971, when the skeletal remains of L&N's once-proud Atlanta–St. Louis *Georgian* arrived for the last time. Georgia Railroad's Atlanta–Augusta, Georgia, run continued operation (Georgia Railroad electing not to join Amtrak), but the train's terminus was moved from Union Station to the Georgia Railroad's Atlanta freight yard office. Union Station was razed and replaced by the Underground Atlanta development early in the 1970s.

A few blocks from Terminal Station, the Georgia Railroad's Atlanta–Augusta accommodation was one of the ten daily trains calling at Atlanta Union Station in early 1968.—JIM BOYD

LOUISVILLE UNION STATION

This compact Romanesque terminal, designed by
architect F. W. Mowbray, was opened by the Louisville &
Nashville Railroad on September 7, 1891. The rusticated
stone head house occupied the block south of Broadway at
the intersection of Tenth Street. The station was noted for
its four square towers—one on each corner—the tallest of
which housed a quartet of clocks. Construction had begun
in 1881, but financial constraints kept the $310,000 pro-
ject from completion for another decade.

The main entrance on Broadway was sheltered by a
metal marquee, above which was a 20-foot-diameter circu-
lar stained glass window. Mowbray made extensive use of
stained glass throughout the station's public areas. A twin

of the front window was located in the waiting room's
south end, and this room's barrel-vaulted ceiling contained
a skylight consisting of 82 square stained-glass panels. A
number of smaller windows continued the colorful theme.
A mosaic floor and wrought-iron balcony railing were
other highlights of the waiting room, in which the station's
ticket office was also located. A barber shop, newsstand,
lunchroom, dining room, lounge, and ladies waiting room
rounded out the ground floor's public areas.

A baggage-and-express annex was located immediately
west of the head house, and beyond that was the terminal's
coach yard. Louisville Union Station's 450-foot-long
clerestoried train shed sheltered six platform tracks, with
umbrella shelters later added to tracks along the shed's west

RIGHT: Stained glass was used prodigiously in Louisville Union Station, both in the head house and, as seen in this late 1960s view, in the train shed.—JIM BOYD

BELOW: By 1975, the train shed was gone. With Amtrak's *Floridian* making its open-air station stop in the background, the Kentucky Railway Museum's restored ex-Monon BL2 No. 32 rested with an excursion consist. Just visible to the right of the station is the Louisville & Nashville's general office building.—MIKE SCHAFER

This southwesterly facing view recorded Nashville Union Station's head house on February 7, 1971. Tracks were depressed below street level, passing under the Broad Street viaduct just visible at right. The station's 200 x 78-foot train shed (out of sight at left) was hemmed in by another viaduct carrying Demonbreun Street across the station tracks and NC&StL's Kayne Ave. yard.—JIM HEUER

side. The terminal hosted trains of owner L&N as well as original tenants Pittsburgh, Cincinnati, Chicago & St. Louis (a Pennsylvania Railroad predecessor) and Chicago, Indianapolis & Louisville (also known as the Monon Route). When the Chesapeake & Ohio vacated Louisville's Central Station in mid-1963, its trains also began using Union Station. The C&O's ever-inventive publicity department drew attention to the move by placing General Passenger Agent James Hamrick, along with his office furniture and a radio telephone, atop a flatbed truck trailer and hauling him through Louisville to Union Station. Dur-

ing the hour-long move, Hamrick promoted special C&O fares to almost 50 telephone callers. Once ensconced at Union Station, the C&O continued its publicity efforts with exhibition trains amid a party atmosphere.

The station that welcomed the C&O in 1963, however, was not entirely the same structure that had opened in 1891. A fire on July 17, 1905, consumed the station's ornate interior and claimed one of the corner towers along with the tallest tower's clocks. The station's stone walls remained, however, and were decreed structurally sound. Within six months, a "new" Union Station had risen from the ashes of the old. Replicating its predecessor in every way, the replacement opened on December 20, 1905, as a remarkable Christmas gift to the people of Louisville.

At the station's peak in the late 1920s, nearly 60 trains were handled every day. Despite the station's proximity to the Ohio River, traffic was disrupted only once by flooding, in 1937. Even as rail passenger traffic experienced a general decline after the Depression, Louisville Union Station could rely on an annual traffic surge the likes of which few other North American terminals ever experienced. For one weekend every May, hundreds of coaches and sleeping cars made their way to Louisville in the consists of both regularly scheduled and extra trains so that their occupants could attend the Kentucky Derby.

Passenger train service to Louisville Union Station ended on October 30, 1976, when Amtrak moved the operation of its *Floridian* to the *Auto-Train* station south of the city. Amtrak shared the new National Turnpike station with *Auto-Train*, operated by a private company which had spun its successful Virginia-to-Florida trains, aboard which passengers and their automobiles traveled together, into an ill-fated Louisville-to-Florida route. The *Auto-Train* and Amtrak's *Floridian* were combined south of Louisville, but by the end of 1979, Amtrak pulled out of Louisville altogether.

The vacated Louisville Union Station was purchased by, and became a hub for bus routes of, the Transit Authority for River City (TARC), sprouting the incongruity of a transit garage. With most of its adjacent trackage removed, the head house received a $2-million renovation in 1979. Particular attention was paid to restoration of the building's stained glass and well as the waiting room's ceramic floor. The renovated structure accommodated offices and a transit museum.

In mid-2000, plans were being developed toward the goal of returning Amtrak service to Louisville and Union Station by extending the new *Kentucky Cardinal* service across the Ohio River from its original 1999 terminus near Jeffersonville, Indiana.

NASHVILLE UNION STATION

On September 3, 1900, the Louisville & Nashville and future merger partner Nashville, Chattanooga & St. Louis Railroad opened their Romanesque terminal in Nashville. The head house occupied a 150-foot x 150-foot space, and was 219 feet tall to the top of its rusticated stone tower. The new station's most prominent exterior feature was topped with a 20-foot-tall bronze statue of Mercury. The likeness had been cast in 1897 for the Tennessee Centennial Exhibition and stood atop the tower until a corroded support caused the statue to fall to its "death" in 1952.

The station's 125 x 67-foot main waiting room, quite appropriately, was finished in Tennessee marble (and oak). Unusual features were the marble fireplaces at each end of the room. The waiting room's three-story high ceiling, like that of its earlier L&N counterpart in Louisville, was graced by a stained-glass skylight. Wall murals depicted Tennessee's riches, while various bas-relief figures added to the station's artistic and esthetic merits.

The ponderous station was a hub for L&N and NC&StL. Famous liners such as the *Humming Bird*, *South Wind*, *Georgian*, *City of Memphis*, and *Pan-American* called at Nashville Union Station. One of the station's claims to fame was that it hosted one of the most complex switching operations in postwar American passenger railroading when, in the small hours of the morning, the *Georgian* from Atlanta met the *Humming Bird* from New Orleans and Memphis and shuffled and exchanged through cars from Atlanta, New Orleans, Memphis, Montgomery, and Mobile destined for Cincinnati, Chicago,

In the final months before Amtrak's arrival, only the *Pan American* and *South Wind* called at Nashville Union Station. This was the southbound *Pan*, making its nocturnal stop on February 6, 1971. This track-level angle shows how the length of the station's clerestoried train shed was restricted by the Demonbreun Street bridge.
—JIM HEUER

LEFT: When this photo was taken of the front of Terminal Station in 1973, it had been transformed into the Chattanooga Choo-Choo and Hilton. Note the style similarities of the station's facade compared to that of the Southern terminal in New Orleans shown on page 110.—MIKE SCHAFER

BELOW: A steam-powered Southern Railway excursion has just arrived at Chattanooga's Terminal Station from Birmingham, Alabama, behind SR 722 in the summer of 1971. By this time, regularly scheduled passenger service had deserted the station.—MIKE SCHAFER

and St. Louis—plus cars originating at Nashville for various points. The process happened in reverse around midnight for the counterpart trains.

Amtrak's Chicago–Florida service continued to call at Nashville Union Station until the *Floridian* was discontinued in 1979. In 1986, the station was redeveloped and opened as the 124-room Union Station Hotel. The station's original character was retained, right down to the vintage arrivals and departures board that serves as a backdrop to the hotel's front desk. A number of rooms open onto the original balcony overlooking the former waiting room.

CHATTANOOGA'S TERMINAL STATION

Long immortalized in song—albeit with considerable license—Chattanooga's Terminal Station is notable as one of the first urban American railroad terminals to be successfully readapted in the absence of its former passenger trains. Opened on December 1, 1909, the station was designed by New York architect Donald Barber and was based on a design-contest entry Barber had executed in 1900 as a student at the l'Ecole des Beaux-Arts in Paris.

Fronting Chattanooga's Market Street between Elyria and Hotel Streets, Barber's compact terminal originally served a dozen stub-ended platform tracks, an adjacent private-car track, and a track dedicated to express loading. A triangular wing behind the south end of the head house accommodated the station's baggage, mail, and express business. Beyond the express wing, an eight-track, 65-car coach yard was connected by a wye track to the station throat and Southern Railway main line.

The terminal's head house was noted for its domed main waiting room, a 62 x 82-foot space under an ornate 85-foot ceiling. Beyond the requisite ticket office, smoking rooms, restaurant, and lunch room, Barber provided passengers with a 300 x 60-foot concourse giving access to the 700-foot-long umbrella-shed platforms.

Terminal Station ended its days as an active passenger train facility on August 11, 1970, when the last remnant of SR's famous *Royal Palm* departed. Vacated by the Southern Railway and facing an uncertain future, the station was subsequently redeveloped as a Hilton hotel property and reopened in 1973. A novel approach to hotel guest accommodation—later emulated by Indianapolis' similarly redeveloped station—saw former sleeping cars permanently parked on the terminal's surviving platform tracks and reconfigured as deluxe suites, two per car. These accommodations were in addition to hotel rooms added inside the

Following its rebirth as part of the Chattanooga Choo-Choo and Hilton Inn, Terminal Station's rotunda (shown in 1973) became a posh dining room.—MIKE SCHAFER

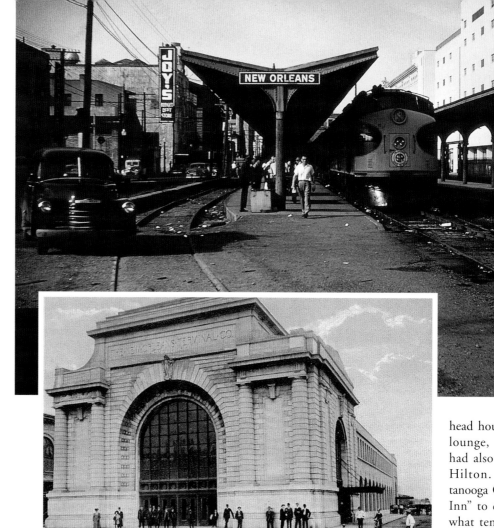

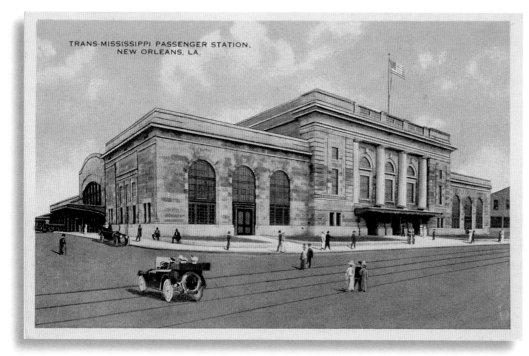

TRANS-MISSISSIPPI PASSENGER STATION. NEW ORLEANS, LA.

head house, into which dining, lounge, and meeting facilities had also been incorporated by Hilton. Named the "Chattanooga Choo Choo and Hilton Inn" to capitalize on its somewhat tenuous connection with the 1941 Glenn Miller recording, the complex enjoyed several years of successful operation with its mix of new attractions including turn-of-the-century-themed retail space, gardens, an electric trolley line serving as a parking lot shuttle, and even a permanent model railroad display. The terminal changed hands again in 1989 as a prelude to a $4-million renovation. This culminated in the hotel's rebranding as a Holiday Inn—noteworthy as one of the few properties in the worldwide chain not purpose-built as a hotel.

NEW ORLEANS

Given the declining fortunes of the American passenger train as the 1950s dawned, New Orleans Union Passenger Terminal is notable as a particularly late attempt at consolidating the operations of outdated existing terminals. This cleanly styled Moderne facility was the result of a 1947 agreement reached by the city and its railroads, with one of the main objectives being grade crossing elimination. NOUPT brought together trains operated by the Texas & New Orleans (an arm of the Southern Pacific); Illinois Central; Gulf, Mobile & Ohio; Southern; Louisiana & Arkansas (a Kansas City Southern subsidiary);

Louisville & Nashville; Missouri Pacific; and Texas & Pacific railroads when it opened in April 1954. NOUPT replaced the former Union Station (IC, T&NO, MP), Canal Street Station (L&N), Terminal Station (SR, GM&O), Rampart Street Station (KCS-L&A), and the T&P-MP facility at Annunciation and Thalia streets.

The stub-ended NOUPT—with its bright, airy, high-ceilinged waiting room—hosted several flagship trains in its brief pre-Amtrak heyday, among them IC's posh *Panama Limited* and fabled *City of New Orleans*, SP's venerable *Sunset Limited*, Southern Railway's *Southerner*, the joint PRR-Southern-A&WP/WofA-L&N *Crescent Limited*, the L&N's *Gulf Wind*, and Texas & Pacific's *Louisiana Eagle*.

NOUPT served Amtrak trains as well as the Southern Railway's *Southern Crescent* from 1971 to 1979, at which time the latter service was taken over by Amtrak and operated as the *Crescent*. Today, the station is a minor Amtrak hub. From Union Passenger Terminal, one can catch the *Crescent* for Birmingham, Atlanta, Washington, or New York; the *City of New Orleans* for Memphis and Chicago; or board the only true transcontinental train in the U. S., the *Sunset Limited*, for points east (Jacksonville and Orlando) and west (Houston and Los Angeles). NOUPT is a multimodal facility, serving bus as well as rail passengers.

One of the station's most unusual claims to fame involves its tracks, which are ballasted with seashells.

Unapologetically Moderne, New Orleans Union Passenger Terminal's facade nonetheless evoked stylized hints of the Beaux Arts colonnade.—KEVIN J. HOLLAND

By 1968, Mopac's presence at **NOUPT** was down to New Orleans-Fort Worth trains 21 and 22.—JIM BOYD

HEADING WEST 6

•St. Paul •Portland • Seattle • Omaha • Denver •Oakland • Kansas City • Dallas • Los Angeles

Although more widely separated than their Eastern counterparts, the railroad terminals of the American West were no less varied. Romanesque, Beaux-Arts, and Art Deco examples were all to be found. In stark contrast to these overtly imported architectural styles, Spanish Colonial (Mission) influences were also seen in terminals of the desert Southwest and California, reaching their zenith in Los Angeles in 1939 with the opening of what many historians have stated to be "the most beautiful railway station in America," Los Angeles Union Passenger Terminal. As was the case in the Southeast, "overhead" tourist traffic was to prove a lucrative revenue source for many Western railroads—particularly those serving California.

By many criteria, a number of terminals featured in this chapter were solidly in America's heartland, specifically St. Paul, Minnesota; Omaha, Nebraska; and Kansas City, Missouri. However, their high status as gateways to the American West—regardless of whether passengers had to change trains there—prompts their inclusion herein.

ST. PAUL UNION DEPOT

Though much a heartland terminal in that numerous Chicago trains originated and terminated here, St. Paul Union Depot was also very much a familiar portal for travelers en route to or from the Pacific Northwest. Begun in August 1917 and completed at a total cost of $15 million, St. Paul Union Depot (SPUD) opened in 1923 to replace a predecessor facility that dated from 1881. One of

SPUD's three principal traffic sources was the lucrative Chicago–Twin Cities market, which became particularly well-contested with the streamlined competition of Chicago, Burlington & Quincy's *Zephyrs*, Chicago & North Western's "*400s*," and Chicago, Milwaukee, St. Paul & Pacific's *Hiawathas*. It was the Twin Cities' approximate distance from Chicago of 400 miles which had, in fact, given the C&NW's fleet its numerical name.

The terminal also served as an important way station for the Chicago–West Coast trains of the Burlington-Great Northern and Burlington-Northern Pacific teams, and The Milwaukee Road. SPUD also hosted regional trains to the likes of northern Minnesota and Michigan, Manitoba, and—via the Chicago, Rock Island & Pacific's *Rocket*s—to more distant points like Fort Worth, Houston, Kansas City, and St. Louis. The *Zephyr Rocket* to the last city was a hybrid joint operation of the CB&Q and Rock Island, and, like the other *Rocket*s serving the Twin Cities, was notable for being essentially a north-south service in a part of the country whose passenger trains were very much oriented on an east-west axis.

In its heyday, nine railroads called at SPUD: North Western; Rock Island; Burlington; Great Northern; Northern

ABOVE: At its peak, St. Paul Union Depot hosted the trains of nine railroads. Only the Minneapolis & St. Louis was missing from this early 1960s ticket blank, which also featured a splendid rendering of the head house.—KEVIN HOLLAND COLLECTION

RIGHT: The pine trees had grown somewhat by the time of this April 29, 1971, view. The following day, SPUD hosted its final passenger trains. Minutes before midnight on Friday, April 30, Burlington Northern's *Afternoon Zephyr* became the last train to use the terminal when it departed for Minneapolis.—JIM HEUER

Pacific; Milwaukee Road; Soo Line; Chicago Great Western; and Minneapolis & St. Louis. Operations within the
terminal itself were under the auspices of the St. Paul
Union Depot Company, created in 1879 and controlled
by the station's occupant railroads.

St. Paul Union Depot's neo-classical Bedford stone
head house was distinguished by its entrance colonnade
facing Fourth and Sibley streets. Inside, a 300 x 100-foot,
three-story main waiting room was finished in Tennessee
travertine and surmounted by a large skylight (later covered). Ticket windows, a restaurant, and railroad

offices—even a bowling alley, a model railroad club, and
GN's preserved *William Crooks* steam locomotive—occupied portions of the head house during the station's life.
Behind the head house, toward the adjacent Mississippi
River, SPUD's 30,000-square-foot train concourse was
built over 17 of the station's 22 through platform tracks.
The station's arrivals and departures board marked the
entrance to the concourse from the waiting room. The
concourse was noted for its skylights and arched, Guastavi-
no-tiled ceiling, as well as for the relief sculptures depicting
the progress of transportation in Minnesota. Passengers

This view, taken early in the afternoon
of July 3, 1968, looks northwest
toward a quiet St. Paul Union Depot.
The track that heads out from the
upper left corner of the station is the
Milwaukee Road to Minneapolis, and
the track that veers away to the left
and across the river is the former
CGW, which had become part of the
C&NW only two days earlier.—ROBERT T.
MC COY, NATE MOLLDREM COLLECTION

could take advantage of additional retail space and another restaurant within the concourse. Unlike its predecessor station, which featured a large train shed, Union Depot's platform tracks were protected by umbrella canopies.

The operation of arriving and departing trains was quite varied. Some railroads backed their trains into SPUD from the wye track at the station's throat while others were able to operate through the depot without reversing direction. C&NW trains from Chicago pulled in, but locomotives were then coupled to the back end of the consists, and the trains pulled backward to Minneapolis. (The city cen-

ters of St. Paul and Minneapolis are only about ten miles apart, so the disorienting journey was short). Trains were often split and combined at SPUD. For example, in later years the *Empire Builder*, *North Coast Limited*, and *Afternoon Zephyr* ran combined as a single train from Chicago to St. Paul. Once at SPUD, they were split apart for GN, NP, and CB&Q to take over their respective sections.

When GN, NP, CB&Q, and Spokane, Portland & Seattle merged on March 2, 1970, SPUD's remaining occupants went from four to two: Milwaukee Road and the newly created Burlington Northern. Serving only 16 trains daily in its final months—down from a peak of over 200 in its earliest years and almost 100 just prior to World War II—SPUD became a casualty of Amtrak's creation and was closed following the departure of BN's Minneapolis-bound *Afternoon Zephyr* that had departed Chicago on April 30, 1971. Amtrak designated the former Great Northern station in Minneapolis as its Twin Cities facility until the new Midway station was built in 1978.

After being vacant for more than a decade, Union Depot was redeveloped beginning in 1981 by the head house's new owner, Asset Development, to accommodate office space and restaurants (the concourse was owned by the Post Office). In addition to its new office and restaurant tenants, Union Depot has hosted art and cultural exhibits.

PORTLAND UNION STATION

Having endured flooding and financial hardship during more than six years of planning and construction, Portland Union Station opened its doors on February 14, 1896. Built by the Union Pacific, Northern Pacific, and Southern Pacific railroads under the auspices of their jointly held Northern Pacific Terminal Company, the $400,000 terminal was designed by the firm of Van Brunt & Howe and was situated on a filled lake bed.

The Italian Renaissance brick, sandstone, and stucco station was termed "the finest west of St. Louis" in contemporary newspaper accounts of its opening. A 144-foot-tall clock tower containing a four-faced timepiece was the station's signature feature.

A decade-long campaign on the part of the Spokane, Portland & Seattle Railway to gain access to Union Station succeeded during World War I, but only through the intervention of the United States Railroad Administration (USRA), the government body which oversaw operation of the country's railroads during and for a short period after the Great War. Despite protestations by Union Station's trio of owning railroads, the SP&S became a permanent tenant in the fall of 1920. Great Northern, which had also been given access to Union Station by the USRA, followed suit by moving its trains into the terminal in June 1922.

With the exception of a mail facility added in 1915, Portland Union Station remained essentially unchanged

Portland's richly textured Union Station as it appeared in 1982. The clock tower—complete with its illuminated lettering—was the station's trademark.—MIKE SCHAFER

until the end of the 1920s, when renovations were made to improve the utility of the building's offices and public areas.

During this time, the station typically accommodated about 90 trains every day; this figure surpassed 100 during World War II's traffic peak. Its owners and tenants brought a remarkably colorful mix of intercity trains to Portland Union Station. These included the Union Pacific's *City of Portland* and *Portland Rose*, as well as the Portland sections of GN's *Empire Builder* and *Western Star* and NP's *North Coast Limited* and *Mainstreeter*, operated via the SP&S to and from Spokane (GN) and Pasco (NP). Portland was the northern terminus of Southern Pacific's Shasta Route up the Pacific Coast from Los Angeles, served by the *Shasta Daylight*, *Cascade*, and *Klamath*. Between Portland and Seattle, the UP, NP, and GN co-ordinated, rather than competed, services on that 186-mile corridor—referring to the operation as the "Pool Trains."

Portland Union Station welcomed Amtrak on May 1, 1971, just over one year after three of its occupants (GN, NP, and SP&S) became part of the Burlington Northern Railroad (along with the Chicago, Burlington & Quincy) on March 2, 1970. Elderly but handsome Portland Union Station remains a busy rail terminal, thanks largely to the success of Amtrak's "Cascadia Corridor," which links Vancouver, British Columbia, and Eugene, Oregon, via Seattle, Tacoma, and Portland. Between the *Cascades*, the Portland section of the *Empire Builder*, and Amtrak's renowned *Coast Starlight*, it is often train time at Portland Union Station.

SEATTLE UNION STATION

By definition, it only took two railroads to make a "union" station. Both of Seattle's twentieth century railroad terminals were, therefore, union stations—curiously, it was the second of this adjacent pair that adopted the description as its official name.

The Northern Pacific and Great Northern railroads had the firm of Reed & Stem design their towered, Italianate King Street Station, which was built facing its namesake thoroughfare between 1904 and 1906. Five years later, and virtually next door, the grandly named Oregon-Washington Railway & Navigation Company (later part of the no-less-grand Union Pacific) opened its "Oregon-Washington Station" on May 20, 1911. Designed by San Francisco architect D. J. Patterson, the O-W facility soon became

Amtrak's Seattle–Chicago *Pioneer*—a direct descendant of Union Pacific's *City of Portland* and its Seattle–Portland Pool Train connection—slips away from Portland Union Station on a blustery February day in 1988. Even in the Amtrak era, Portland Union Station remains a busy passenger terminal, thanks to the growth in the Vancouver–Seattle–Portland–Eugene corridor.—MIKE SCHAFER

known as Union Station, since it also handled the Pacific Coast trains of the newly completed Puget Sound extension of the Chicago, Milwaukee, St. Paul & Pacific.

The structure exhibited subdued elements of Beaux Arts styling in its decidedly uncharacteristic brick and stone exterior. Inside, the terminal's most prominent feature was its tile-floored, 55-foot high, barrel-vaulted main waiting room, the ceiling punctuated with a skylight and decorative medallions. This space was entered through a vestibule from the station's main Jackson Street entrance, and was surrounded by all of the "usual" services of its day: a ticket office; baggage checking; ladies waiting room; smoking room; barber shop; and newsstand. All of these facilities were at street level; the stub-ended station tracks lay 24 feet below, with passenger access via stairs from the 40-foot-wide concourse. The head house's lower lever contained baggage-handling facilities, a compact hospital, and an immigrant waiting area.

After July 5, 1927, the Milwaukee Road's presence gave Seattle Union Station membership in an exclusive club—at least in North American terms—comprising urban terminals with electrified mainline operations. That date marked the completion of the final, short stretch of the Milwaukee's mainline electrification, the approximately ten miles between Seattle Union Station and Black River Junction.

Even with the operational efficiencies of electrification, however, Milwaukee trains were obliged to follow a convoluted path into and out of Union Station as they traveled between Tacoma and the east. Arriving from the east, the Milwaukee's trains headed straight into Union Station after leaving the main line at Black River Junction. Once in the station, the electric "motor" would run around its train and, at the appointed hour, pull the consist backward back out to the junction and on to Tacoma. Eastbound runs did this backward run in reverse, with the train properly pointed upon departure from Seattle.

This pre-1927 view of Seattle Union Station faces southeast and illustrates how the surrounding streets were supported above track level. After July 1927, the station tracks were electrified, employing overhead wire, marking completion of the Milwaukee Road's mainline electrification project. Above the station's main entrance were the inscriptions "UNION PACIFIC— C.M.&ST.P.RY." and "UNION STATION."
—MILWAUKEE ROAD PHOTO, MILWAUKEE ROAD HISTORICAL ASSOCIATION

Union Station was notable as a home for some rather unorthodox equipment after World War II. Union Pacific purchased Pullman-Standard's *Train of Tomorrow* consist, and these pioneering dome cars ran between Seattle and Portland for years. In 1948–49 The Milwaukee Road added Skytop sleeper-lounge observation cars to its new (1947) *Olympian Hiawatha*; in 1952 the *Olympian Hi* received full-length "Super Domes." This riot of exotica was short-lived, however, as Milwaukee Road ended its passenger service to Washington state on May 23, 1961. Union Station hosted its final train almost exactly a decade later, as UP's last Portland local departed and Amtrak consolidated its Seattle operations at King Street Station.

Remarkably, Seattle Union Station survived to embrace a new life in 1999 as the headquarters of Sound Transit, operators of regional mass transportation including "Sounder" heavy rail commuter trains (which, ironically, serve Seattle from King Street Station). Union Station underwent a multi-million dollar restoration and conversion for its new use, yet retained some of its former public spaces to accommodate special functions and events.

OMAHA UNION STATION

This Art Deco nugget opened on January 15, 1931, replacing an earlier Union Station on the same site, approximately a half-mile west of the Missouri River. The project's $3.5 million budget included approximately $50,000 for a temporary 436 x 50-foot wooden station, built in less than 90 days in the summer of 1929 to bridge the gap between the demolition of the old station and the opening of the new facility. The new station's pale cream glazed terra-cotta exterior—dramatically spotlit at night—and ornamentation was designed by Los Angeles architect Gilbert S. Underwood and was a stylistic counterpoint to the similarly proportioned but decidedly neo-classical Burlington station located just a few hundred yards to the south. The CB&Q had opted out of participation in the earlier Union Station and its 1931 replacement for financial reasons, instead choosing to renovate and radically restyle its existing 1898 station.

Omaha Union Station was built as an "island" abutting the city's Tenth Street viaduct and was located next to the tracks of the Union Pacific Railroad. The station's other

A 1965 aerial view of Seattle Union Station and its towered neighbor, King Street Station. Union was essentially a stub-end terminal, although one platform track reached northward along the east side of the head house, passed under the street, and dead-ended. Toward the end of this track was a switch leading to an "escape" track. This arrangement allowed an arriving train's locomotive to be cut off and run around the train—a necessity for the Milwaukee Road, whose trains did not terminate or originate at the station, but passed through.—ROBERT MC COY, NATE MOLLDREM COLLECTION

occupants included Chicago & North Western and subsidiary Chicago, St. Paul, Minneapolis & Omaha ("the Omaha Road"), Chicago Great Western, Rock Island, Milwaukee Road, Missouri Pacific, Illinois Central, and Wabash, all of whom were obliged to enter the terminal over UP rails.

The new station's facade fronted a 110-car parking ramp, with paired station entrances denoted by heavy rectangular marquees. These were topped, as was the Tenth Street entrance, with relief sculptures of railroad workers and their tools. Underwood's stated goal in the station's design was "to express the distinctive character of the railroad—strength, power, masculinity." The head house was effectively divided into thirds, with the 160 x 72-foot x 60-foot-high waiting room and ticket office occupying the center portion.

Simulated marble finishes were Underwood's choice of interior decor in the waiting room, with a sculpted plaster ceiling, geometric-patterned terrazzo floor, Caen stone walls, and oak trim. Natural light was admitted through ten colored-glass windows, with artificial illumination provided most obviously by six 13-foot-high, 5-foot-diameter bronze and glass Art Deco chandeliers. The eastern third of the station, farthest from the street, contained baggage checking facilities, a newsstand, and a restaurant and lunch counter. Highlighting the restaurant's decor were murals on the east and west walls, executed by Los Angeles artist Joseph W. Keller in 1930 and depicting the evolution of transportation—a recurring theme in station murals. Underwood continued his fondness for faux-finishes in this part of the station, with simulated marble floors and imitation travertine walls.

The western third, with access to Tenth Street, contained men's and women's rooms, telephones, a medical room, a barber shop, and the stationmaster's office. Express and baggage facilities were located at track level, with vehicular access via a long ramp from the viaduct. Much of the station's office space was also located below street level. A narrow concourse area opened off of the south side of the waiting room, and through this passengers could either descend to track level or reach an enclosed walkway connecting to the nearby Burlington station. On the strength of the trains operated via the "Overland Route" between Chicago and various points on the West Coast, Omaha Union Station actually saw the number of daily trains increase through the late 1930s and into the early postwar years—to a high of 80 in 1947, up from an original 45.

Omaha-based UP was the middle partner in the Overland Route triumvirate, and the yellow *City* streamliners were the celebrities of Union Station's arrivals and departures board. C&NW relayed the trains between Chicago and Omaha until October 1955 when that duty was shifted to The Milwaukee Road.

Union Station, Omaha, Neb.

The original Omaha Union Station is shown in this postcard postmarked (at Denver Union Station, no less) on St. Valentine's Day 1911. The view—a colorized black-and-white photo—looks southeast, and Union Pacific's Missouri River bridge can be seen in the distance. This building was demolished in 1929 to make way for the new Union Station (below).—MIKE SCHAFER COLLECTION

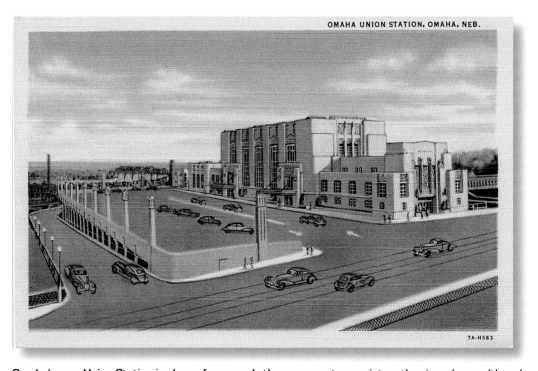

OMAHA UNION STATION, OMAHA, NEB.

Omaha's new Union Station is shown from nearly the same vantage point as the view above, although artistic license has resulted in some heavy retouching on its surroundings (it appears the automobiles were added as an afterthought). UP's new bridge over the Missouri River can be seen in the distance. The exterior of the depot remains essentially unchanged today.—KIM TSCHUDY COLLECTION

Even as overall traffic increased prior to the war, however, Union Station lost its first (and admittedly marginal) occupant when Illinois Central discontinued the Omaha section of its Chicago–Sioux City, Iowa, *Hawkeye* in 1939. Stability reigned until 1958, when C&NW retrenched across the Missouri River to Council Bluffs, Iowa—a move duplicated by Wabash in 1960. MP exited Union Station in 1965, followed by CGW 20 days later. Rock Island pulled out in 1969. On the eve of Amtrak, only Union Pacific and Milwaukee Road remained at Union Station, with a single consolidated Chicago–West Coast train mockingly dubbed the "City of Everywhere"—a reference to the once-separate *City of San Francisco, City of Los Angeles, Challenger, City of Denver,* and *City of Portland* domeliners that it replaced. The Milwaukee's own trains—the Chicago–Omaha/Sioux Falls *Midwest Hiawatha* and the *Arrow*—had bowed out in 1956 and 1967 respectively.

Following departure of the last *City* train on May 2, 1971, Omaha Union Station was closed. Amtrak made its Omaha debut in the Burlington station, and UP donated Omaha Union Station to the city in 1973. For a period in 1977 and 1978, Amtrak considered vacating the old CB&Q facility in favor of the mothballed Union Station, but those plans were dropped and a new Amtrak station was built nearby beginning in late 1983. In the meantime, Omaha Union Station was redeveloped and survives as the Western Heritage Museum, which opened in 1975

DENVER UNION STATION

The casual observer could reasonably conclude that Denver has had three distinct union stations—reasonably, and not entirely incorrectly. In fact, the sprawling structure erected by financier Jay Gould to serve "his" railroads

in 1881 has undergone a remarkable metamorphosis—not once, but twice. As the 1870s drew to a close, Gould controlled all nine of the railroads then serving the state of Colorado. Five of these in turn entered Denver, whose citizens were obliged to juggle their travels between five separate passenger terminals. Gould's solution, at once self-serving and magnanimous, was to organize the Union Depot & Railroad Company for the purposes of establishing a consolidated passenger terminal in the city. Self-serving, because Gould profited handsomely from the exercise; magnanimous, because the efficiencies and convenience of a union terminal were obvious to passengers and railroads alike.

The original Denver Union Depot, designed by architect W. E. Taylor and officially opened on June 1, 1881, had steep dormered and clerestoried roofs surmounting its pink and gray granite walls. The 504-foot long structure's Flemish overtones would have been equally at home in Antwerp or Amsterdam: the station's street side, fronting Wynkoop Street and terminating the vista down what became 17th Street, had the hallmarks of a European streetscape. Seven distinct sections created the illusion of individual buildings, punctuated at the center by an elaborate 230-foot clock tower. The design of the station's track side, while less ornate, was still consistent. Additional single-story wings were built on both ends of the original structure in 1892, two years before tragedy struck in the form of a devastating fire. Leaving only the heavy stone walls standing, the March 18, 1894, fire devastated the clock tower and entire southern portion of the station. Union Depot's second incarnation came when the structure was rebuilt within its original walls, but with a new clock tower and a low-profile roof with squat horizontal dormers.

Union Depot's appearance was unchanged for the next two decades, until 1912 when the structure's center section and 1894 clock tower gave way to a curiously Italianate gray granite replacement. The new centerpiece marked the station's third iteration, and was neatly grafted between the previously reroofed 1881 north and south wings. Coincident with completion of the new addition in 1914, the Union Depot & Railway Co. was reorganized as the Denver Union Terminal Railway Company (DUTCo), and the terminal itself renamed Denver Union Station. The new DUTCo was owned by the railroads then serving the station: Denver & Rio Grande; Rock Island; Santa Fe; Burlington; Colorado & Southern; and Union Pacific. Ultimate control rested with UP. Until April 1937, Denver Union Station was remarkable among urban North American terminals for hosting trains operating on two track gauges—standard (4 feet 8$\frac{1}{2}$ inches between the rails) and 36-inch narrow gauge. For 56 years prior to the discontinuance of the Colorado & Southern's last narrow-gauge train, all of the terminal's trackage was

Denver Union Station's 1912 center block stood in marked contrast to the terminal's north and south wings, which traced their origins to 1892. Their low-profile roofline was the result of an 1894 fire. In this September 1969 scene, Burlington's *Denver Zephyr* rests at the platform with business car *The Round-Up* carrying the marker lights.—A.M. LANGLEY, JR.

dual-gauge, with a third rail inside the standard gauge to accommodate the narrow-gauge equipment.

Union Station's best-known and most fondly remembered visitor was the original *California Zephyr*, a dome-bejeweled stainless-steel "cruise" train geared primarily to tourists and jointly operated between Chicago and Oakland by the CB&Q, Rio Grande, and Western Pacific railroads. The *CZ* was launched in 1949, ten years after its largely heavyweight predecessor, the *Exposition Flyer*, had made news as the first train to operate through Denver Union Station rather than terminating there (although the train had to back in upon arrival). Union Pacific's *City of Kansas City* and, for a short time, *City of Portland* later shared that claim.

Prominent among the station's postwar schedules were examples of some of America's best-known passenger train fleets. Rock Island's *Rocket*s, Missouri Pacific's *Eagle*s, Burlington's *Zephyr*s, and Union Pacific's *City* trains all were represented at Denver until the mid-1960s. In 1965 the MP and Rock Island terminated their passenger services to Denver, and Burlington subsidiary C&S followed suit in 1967. Stalwarts UP, CB&Q, Rio Grande, and Santa Fe nonetheless oversaw the attrition of their Denver schedules through the second half of the decade, playing out the same story seen throughout the U.S. at the time.

By the time of Amtrak's 1971 debut, even the fabled *California Zephyr* had disappeared as a through train. The Rio Grande's status as an Amtrak non-member meant that

The street side of Denver Union Station's center block—shown here in 1969—exhibits Italianate influences shared with Chicago's North Western Terminal.—JIM HEUER

a tri-weekly service, the *Rio Grande Zephyr* (arguably Denver Union Station's *second* most fondly remembered inhabitant) persisted over the railroad's portion of the former *CZ* route from 1970 until 1983. At that time, Amtrak reinstated the *California Zephyr* name with a re-routed Chicago–Oakland Superliner schedule, replacing the *RGZ*. Rio Grande and successor Southern Pacific, meanwhile, maintained a seasonal presence in the station with their seasonal *Ski Train* operation to the resort area of Winter Park. A redevelopment of the area around the terminal resulted in some operational changes. The adjacent freight main line was relocated away from the station district and Union Station itself transformed into a stub-end facility. In mid-2000, DUS was the subject of redevelopment proposals that sought its inclusion in a light-rail network serving the Central Platte Valley and, potentially, Denver's airport.

With the Front Range of the Rockies rising in the distance, the *California Zephyr*—missing one of its usual complement of domes—departs Denver in the summer of 1969. This view illustrates the contrast in size and style between the station's center block and its older end wings.—JIM HEUER

OAKLAND PIER

Known by its unappealing yet descriptive nickname of the "Mole" (actually a term for any earth-and-stone pier), Southern Pacific's Oakland Pier terminal opened in 1882 at the end of a long fill extending into San Francisco Bay. The Mole served as a connection point between SP's intercity trains and Oakland commuter operations, to the east, and the railroad's cross-bay ferries to and from San Francisco, on the west. Oakland Pier's suburban trains took the form, after 1911, of "Red Electric" interurban-type cars. In 1939 the electrics gained direct access to San Francisco via the newly opened double-deck, vehicular/rail Oakland–San Francisco Bay Bridge, and vacated the Mole.

In its prime, the SP's Oakland Pier handled over 750 daily movements on its 20 stub-ended tracks, with most of these trains made up of Red Electrics whose schedules were

Wreathed in its own exhaust, Southern Pacific train 52, the *San Joaquin Daylight*, departs the Oakland Pier on a gloomy morning in 1955.—ROBERT O. HALE; JAY WILLIAMS COLLECTION

coordinated with those of the ferries. Almost 60,000 passengers a day passed through the Mole in its heyday between the World Wars. Santa Fe trains used the Mole between 1918 and 1920, and a more permanent tenant moved in during the Depression.

The Western Pacific Railroad had operated its own "mole" and cross-bay ferry terminal a short distance south of Southern Pacific's Oakland Pier since reaching Oakland in 1909. In the 1930s, the cash-strapped WP reached an arrangement with SP to operate its trains out of the latter's station and share a single cross-bay ferry operation. When Western Pacific—along with partners Chicago, Burlington & Quincy and Denver & Rio Grande Western—launched the *California Zephyr* in March 1949, SP's Oakland Pier became the celebrated train's first western terminus, despite a pre-inaugural consist having been displayed on San Francisco's Embarcadero to whet that city's appetite. WP's Budd Rail Diesel Car companion train, the *Zephyrette*, mingled with SP's own RDCs under the Pier's arched train shed until WP removed its trains from the SP terminal upon the cessation of ferry service in July 1958. After that, the famed *CZ* originated at a dedicated track in WP's Oakland freight yard.

Passengers crossing the Bay to and from San Francisco's Ferry Building were accommodated aboard SP's trio of nineteenth century vessels: the paddle-wheelers *Sacramento* and *Eureka*, and the newer, screw-equipped *Berkeley*. The *Sacramento* was replaced by the *San Leandro* in 1954, and the *Eureka* was retired three years later.

The *CZ* may have been Oakland Pier's stainless-steel celebrity, but it was only one train against the SP's multiple

postwar offerings. The *Shasta Daylight, Cascade, Oakland Lark, City of San Francisco*, and even the head-end-heavy *Klamath* were all streamliners of note in their own right, clad in schemes ranging from SP's vibrant "Daylight" red and orange or "Overland Route" yellow to somber grays.

The Oakland Pier closed on March 24, 1960, and SP began terminating its intercity runs at its 16th Street Station in Oakland. Soon after, the Mole was demolished. The ferry *Eureka* is preserved as part of a maritime museum across the Bay at Fisherman's Wharf, and farther down the Pacific coast in San Diego, the *Eureka*'s sister vessel, the *Berkeley*, also survives in retirement.

In another 1950s view of train 52 at the Mole, GS-4 No. 4455 awaits the train's 7:53 am departure and 478-mile inland trek to Los Angeles.
—RAILROAD AVENUE ENTERPRISES, ANDOVER JUNCTION PUBLICATIONS COLLECTION

KANSAS CITY UNION STATION

In a railroad context, Kansas City has much in common with Chicago. Both mark transitions between east and west. Both had sprawling stockyard facilities, and both once counted their trunk line railroads in double digits. An important distinction between the two was the ability of Kansas City's railroad interests to cooperate on a union station project—not once, but twice—in stark contrast to the fragmented and fractious situation in Chicago (Chapter 4) that in a sense lasts to this day. Kansas City Union Station was so enormous, in fact, that it was the third-largest passenger terminal in the U.S. when it opened. Only New York City's two great terminals were bigger.

KCUS opened on October 31, 1914. The arrival of that day's Missouri-Kansas-Texas (MKT) *Katy Flyer* marked the culmination of an eight-year project undertaken by a dozen railroads to replace the city's 1878 Union Depot. The old station in the city's West Bottoms district was, even by the turn of the twentieth century, hopelessly inadequate in the face of Kansas City's growing population and burgeoning rail traffic. Not the least of Union Depot's problems was its location on a flood plain. A week-long disruption in service caused by a 1903 flood of the Kansas

(also known as the Kaw) and Missouri rivers was the last straw for the railroads serving the depot, and the search was on for a site for a new "union" station.

By mid-1906, the city's 12 trunk railroads had formed the Kansas City Terminal Railway Company (ownership of which was equally shared) and had agreed upon a location for the new facility, just south of city center. Key selection criteria included reduced vulnerability to flooding, along with space to accommodate more extensive platform and approach trackage than was possible at the old Union Depot site. The railroads also settled upon an architect for the project: Jarvis Hunt (1859–1941) of Chicago. Hunt won the commission in 1906 with plans reflecting his adherence to the City Beautiful movement—his $11-million Kansas City Union Station would be a monumental facility in both size and Beaux Arts style.

Hunt sheathed his 150 x 510-foot head house in Bedford stone and granite. The waiting room and midway portion of the station, located over the platform tracks, measured 165 x 410 feet, of which the main waiting room itself occupied 78 x 352 feet. The Great Hall was a 92-foot high space, measuring 103 x 242 feet, with its floor area unencumbered save for the semicircular intrusion of a ticket sales area beneath one of the three large arched windows. The station's through tracks were depressed below street level and reached by stairways from the concourse.

Alas, like so many of its contemporaries, the facility peaked early. More trains passed through Kansas City Union Station in 1917—79,368—than would do so in any other year. As many as 271 trains a day called at KCUS that year. Union Station made headlines in June 1933 as the scene of the "Kansas City Massacre," a deadly confrontation between gangsters and law officers outside the station's east entrance. Five agents died in a hail of bullets as a trio of gunmen attempted to free Frank Nash, a prison escapee being returned under guard to Leavenworth, Kansas. Ironically, Nash also died in the ambush. The bullet marks are still visible on the depot building.

By virtue of the diverse mix of railroads that it served, KCUS would figure in rather more positive headlines through the balance of the 1930s. Streamlined, lightweight, articulated trains were becoming the fashion as railroads sought to hold their ground against the automobile's inroads. Two of the earliest proponents of the new technology—Chicago, Burlington & Quincy and Union Pacific—served Kansas City, and Union Station was an early host to their futuristic efforts. Following a nationwide barnstorming tour, Burlington's stainless-steel, shovel-nosed *Zephyr* 9900 debuted in revenue service on November 11, 1934, between Kansas City and Lincoln, Nebraska. UP's wormlike M-10000 made its first Kansas City–Salina, Kansas, trip on January 31, 1935, as *The Streamliner*.

107—Grand Lobby, Union Station, Kansas City, Mo.

Kansas City Union Station's fortunes mirrored those of other major passenger terminals across the country. Even this huge facility was strained by the volume of World War II traffic. Half of America's armed forces personnel reportedly passed through the station during the course of the conflict. Although 1917 witnessed the greatest number of trains serving Union Station, more passengers passed

The Grand Lobby of Kansas City Union Station. Ticket offices occupied the semi-circular intrusion at right. Access to the main waiting room and midways was through the passage at left. Beyond the ticket office in this postcard view were an information kiosk, the Fred Harvey restaurant, and a women's waiting room.—PHIL AND BEV BIRK COLLECTION

Santa Fe's *Kansas Cityan*, train 11, will depart its namesake for Dallas in the summer of 1965 as soon as switching of through cars received from Chicago via the *Chief* is complete. General Motors E8s were a relative rarity on the Santa Fe—a railroad known far and wide for its fleet of "Warbonnet" F-units—but they generally worked between Chicago, Kansas City, and Dallas on the *Chief*, *Kansas Cityan*, and *Chicagoan*.—MIKE MC BRIDE

ABOVE: Shorn of its train sheds, KCUS is in its twilight years as a true railroad station in this night scene recorded during the small hours of January 1, 1975. At left, Amtrak's Chicago–Los Angeles *Southwest Limited* awaits its appointed departure time after setting out a chartered sleeping car (center) from Chicago carrying a group of National Railway Historical Society travelers celebrating the new year in style. At right, retired former CB&Q *Texas Zephyr* equipment awaits an uncertain fate.—MIKE SCHAFER

LEFT: Switching within the confines of Kansas City Union Station was handled by the Kansas City Terminal Railway. KCT Alco S-2 No. 52 was working a head-end cut in the summer of 1965.—MIKE MC BRIDE

through in 1945 than ever before or since. Union Station did its share for victory, only to face a relentless decline in the number of passengers, trains, and railroads themselves through the 1950s and 1960s. The first railroad to discontinue service to Kansas City was The Milwaukee Road, in 1958. Gulf, Mobile & Ohio pulled out in 1960 with the final arrival of its motorcar run from Bloomington, Illinois, and Chicago Great Western followed suit in 1962. St. Louis-San Francisco (Frisco) ended service in 1967, and by the end of 1969, Rock Island, Kansas City Southern, and Wabash successor Norfolk & Western had all departed. As

was the case with Omaha Union Station, some railroads retrenched their services to nearby freight facilities. Under new management unsympathetic to the plight of the passenger train, Burlington shifted its four remaining K.C. passenger trains to one of its Kansas City freight yards in 1970; similarly, UP moved a couple of its trains to nearby freight facilities.

After the debut of Amtrak on May 1, 1971, Kansas City Union Station hosted a mere six trains a day. As the curtain fell on the era of privately operated passenger trains through the first four months of that year, the station had

All of Kansas City Union Station is splayed out in this 1970 view that looks northeast. Plainly evident are the station's head house, the east and west wings, and the concourse building over the platform tracks; at lower left is the Railway Express Agency's facility. Mainline freight operations bypassed the station just to the north.—ROBERT T. MC COY PHOTO, NATE MOLLDREM COLLECTION

In the spring of 1981, Jarvis Hunt's Dallas Union Station head house offered an elegant contrast to a pair of the city's latter-day architectural adornments.—MIKE SCHAFER

echoed to three times as many trains, operated by a trio of stalwart railroads—Union Pacific, Missouri Pacific, and Santa Fe. Only two decades earlier, over 100 trains in the colors of 12 railroads (CB&Q, AT&SF, UP, MP, MKT, KCS, CRI&P, CGW, CMStP&P, GM&O, SLSF, and WAB) had called at KCUS every day.

Although unattractive yet cost-effective drop ceilings and partitions helped Amtrak curb the exorbitant heating and lighting expenses in many of its large inherited terminals, in Kansas City the carrier took the bizarre step of cocooning its station functions within an inflated vinyl chamber in a corner of the Grand Hall. This "bubble," as it came to be known, survived until Amtrak opened a nondescript block structure beneath the adjacent Main Street

viaduct in 1985. Purchased by a Canadian real-estate development company in 1974, Kansas City Union Station languished—but survived (except for its train sheds)—until the Union Station Assistance Corporation took over the property and formulated plans for its future. Taking a cue from similar renewal efforts in Cincinnati, the station emerged as part of the $250-million "Science City at Union Station" complex in 1999.

DALLAS UNION STATION

This white-brick neo-classical structure was another true "union" station, opened in 1916 to replace a half-dozen predecessors in the wake of spirited pressure from civic and state leaders and the *Dallas Morning News*.

The city's eight railroads, initially resistant to the idea of a shared station facility, acquiesced with the 1912 formation of the jointly held Dallas Union Terminal Company. The commission for the terminal's design was awarded to architect Jarvis Hunt, fresh from his work on Kansas City's Union Station. Ground was broken for Dallas Union Station on February 2, 1914, and the $6.4-million complex handled its first revenue train on October 8, 1916. An official opening ceremony followed six days later.

The station's nine original through platform tracks, protected by umbrella canopies and reached from the station via an overhead concourse, were designed to accommodate approximately 100 daily trains—a figure exceeded only during World War II. Traffic was controlled by interlocking towers at the station's north and south throats, while an adjacent locomotive terminal and 85-car coach yard accommodated equipment servicing and layover. Baggage, mail, and express facilities flanked the station building, with this head-end business originally reaching the trains by of overhead structures similar to the passenger concourse.

The terminal's three-story head house contained a 128 x 70-foot x 45-foot high main waiting room, flanked by restaurants and the train concourse. Rather oddly, all of these spaces were located on the building's second floor, one flight up from the main Houston Street entrance and the ticketing area. The station's third floor provided office space for railroads and related tenants. The awkward "up-and-down" pedestrian flow was improved somewhat in 1946 with the installation of escalators and a tunnel. The overhead concourse was removed completely in 1973.

As would be expected, the convergence of passenger trains operated by eight major railroads made Dallas Union Terminal a vibrant facility, particularly during the colorful post–World War II "streamline era." The red, yellow, and stainless steel of Santa Fe; the orange and red

Purchased by the City of Dallas in 1973, Union Station is today served by Amtrak and DART, Dallas' rail transit operator. Under city ownership, the main waiting room was adapted to restaurant use, as in this 1981 view.
—MIKE SCHAFER

A Cotton Belt train receives attention on one of Dallas Union Station's platform tracks, circa 1938. A portion of the elevated concourse is visible above the consist. That portion of the terminal was razed in 1973.—OTTO PERRY; DENVER PUBLIC LIBRARY COLLECTION

"Daylight" hues of Southern Pacific subsidiary Texas & New Orleans; Missouri Pacific and affiliate Texas & Pacific's rich blue and gray; the varied reds of Rock Island, Frisco, and Missouri-Kansas-Texas; the somber green of Pullman heavyweight sleepers; and the virtually unadorned stainless-steel counterpoint of Burlington subsidiary Fort Worth & Denver all contributed to Dallas' spectrum.

Switching operations were the purview of the Terminal Company, which kept a small fleet of steam and, later, diesel locomotives busy in this assignment—remarkably, a steam engine survived in this role until mid-1961, long after the terminal's mainline trains (and those throughout the rest of North America) had been dieselized.

America's postwar "age of innocence" came to a bloody end in Dallas on November 22, 1963, with Union Station an unfortunate backdrop. As President John F. Kennedy's motorcade passed Dealey Plaza—named in honor of the *Dallas Morning News* publisher who had so strongly advocated Union Station's construction—events unfolded in the shadow of the station's north throat underpass that would be forever etched in the memories of millions worldwide. Dallas Union Station tower operators were among the hundreds questioned by investigators of the Kennedy assassination.

The nation's century old dependence upon the passenger train was also coming to an abrupt end during the early 1960s, as travelers opted for government-sponsored improved roads and airline service, and the U. S. Post Office accelerated the withdrawal of its lucrative mail-carrying contracts. Dallas Union Station's decline was more precipitous than many of its urban counterparts, for in 1969 the station and the city found themselves bereft of any rail passenger service when Missouri Pacific's Fort Worth–New Orleans segment—train Nos. 21 and 22—of the once far-flung *Texas Eagle* network called at DUS for the final time. Not long before, Santa Fe had exited Dallas with the wholesale discontinuance of a cluster of Dallas operations that included its Dallas–Chicago *Chicagoan*, the Kansas City–Dallas *Kansas Cityan*, and the Dallas section of the Chicago–Houston *Texas Chief*. When MP pulled out, Dallas suddenly acquired the dubious honor of being the largest population center in North America without rail passenger service.

Almost three years passed after Amtrak's 1971 creation before the new passenger carrier was in a position to restore passenger rail service to Dallas. After a five-year hiatus, Dallas Union Station again welcomed a passenger train when Amtrak extended its Laredo–Fort Worth *Inter-American* on to St. Louis via Dallas on March 14, 1974. Amtrak has maintained a checkered presence at the terminal, most recently with its daily Superliner *Texas Eagle*. The facility again became a "union" station in December 1996 with the inauguration of Dallas Area Rapid Transit (DART) light-rail and heavy-rail commuter services. Owned by the city since 1973, the renovated station's head house caters to passengers with ticketing and waiting areas in the former first-floor ticket lobby, while the main waiting room was converted to a restaurant.

Los Angeles Union Passenger Terminal

Like its slightly older Midwestern counterpart in Cincinnati, Los Angeles Union Passenger Terminal (LAUPT) is an idiosyncratic jewel among North America's classic railway stations. Architecturally, the two are as diverse as any pair of like-purposed structures could be. While Cincinnati's Art Deco masterpiece figuratively leaps from its subdued surroundings, LAUPT's hybrid of Spanish Colonial Revival (Mission) and Art Deco styling influences seems very much at home in the City of Angels, just as the terminal's creators intended.

Generally conceded to be the last in the lineage of North America's landmark urban railroad terminals, the $11-million LAUPT's May 7, 1939, official opening was preceded by great celebration between May 3 and May 5. The new station consolidated the passenger train operations of Santa Fe, Southern Pacific, and Union Pacific in a city enjoying its heyday as the self-proclaimed capital of the motion-picture industry (the year 1939 also saw the debut of such cinema classics as "Gone With the Wind" and "The Wizard of Oz") and, not entirely unrelated, as an emerging destination for tourists and migrants alike. And what finer place for UP's new 1939-edition *City of Los Angeles* to call home than Los Angeles Union Passenger Terminal?

The new LAUPT was seen by civic leaders as a destination whose architecture should embody the essence of Southern California. Contemporary promotional literature described the design as having "streamlined the pueblo, creating a functionally modern facility that was architecturally beautiful and typically Californian." The terminal complex occupied 48 acres bounded by Alameda Street on the west, Macy Street on the north, and Aliso Street on the south. The head house itself, with its signature clock tower, had an 850-foot facade fronting Alameda Street.

Designed by Donald and John Parkinson (who were also responsible for Los Angeles' City Hall and Bullock's Wilshire department store), the terminal's cruciform plan incorporated a soaring main waiting room and adjacent

continued on page 136

Los Angeles Union Passenger Terminal's clock tower—like the rest of the structure, a highbred of Colonial Revival (Mission) and Art Deco styling—rises above the lushly landscaped grounds in May 1973. The station's design took advantage of Southern California climes, with several outdoor plazas where travelers could soak up the sun while awaiting boarding announcements for the *Super Chief, Coast Daylight, City of Los Angeles* and other famous flagships that called LAUPT their home.—MIKE SCHAFER

9A-H918

Eclectic styling was to be found inside **LAUPT** as well. This postcard recorded the main waiting room, with its leather settees and intricate ceiling. Note that the passengers have focused their attention on the postcard photographer.—KEVIN HOLLAND COLLECTION

RIGHT: **LAUPT** celebrated its 50th birthday in May 1989, making every bit the architectural statement of its opening half a century before.—JIM BOYD

ABOVE: As seen in this February 1981 view, **LAUPT**'s architects embraced the city's semi-tropical climate by providing passengers with the option of outdoor waiting areas, complete with tiled benches, fountains, and gardens.—MIKE SCHAFER

Continued from page 133

With its timbered ceilings and wrought-iron grillework, LAUPT's ticket concourse—photographed in February 1981—reflected the architect's desire to capture "an atmosphere of tranquility" and to pay tribute to the "tradition of the Californians of days gone by."—MIKE SCHAFER

ticket hall, both of which featured intricately painted timber-framed ceilings. Cork paneling on the interior walls improved the rooms' acoustics. Mosaic floors were laid with Montana travertine and marble from sources as diverse as Vermont, Tennessee, Spain, Belgium, and France. More marble was incorporated in wainscots and borders, along with tile and travertine. In the main waiting room, rows of leather-upholstered settees flanked a central aisle. Accents were executed in American Black Walnut, as well as wrought iron, bronze, and satin-finish aluminum.

Taking advantage of the city's natural, warm climate, the Parkinsons also provided open-air waiting areas complete with ceramic-tiled fountains and benches. Two such patios, one on either side of the main waiting room, echoed the lavish landscaping of the entire complex, which featured orange trees, palm trees, olive trees, and pepper trees along with native shrubs and flowers. A Fred Harvey dining room was located south of the terminal's main entrance, along with a cocktail lounge, while a barber shop and newsstand were accessible from the ticket hall.

The Santa Fe, Southern Pacific, and Union Pacific railroads were justifiably proud of their new Los Angeles landmark. This 1939 brochure was issued to introduce the new terminal and familiarize visitors and Angelenos alike with its features.
—KEVIN HOLLAND COLLECTION

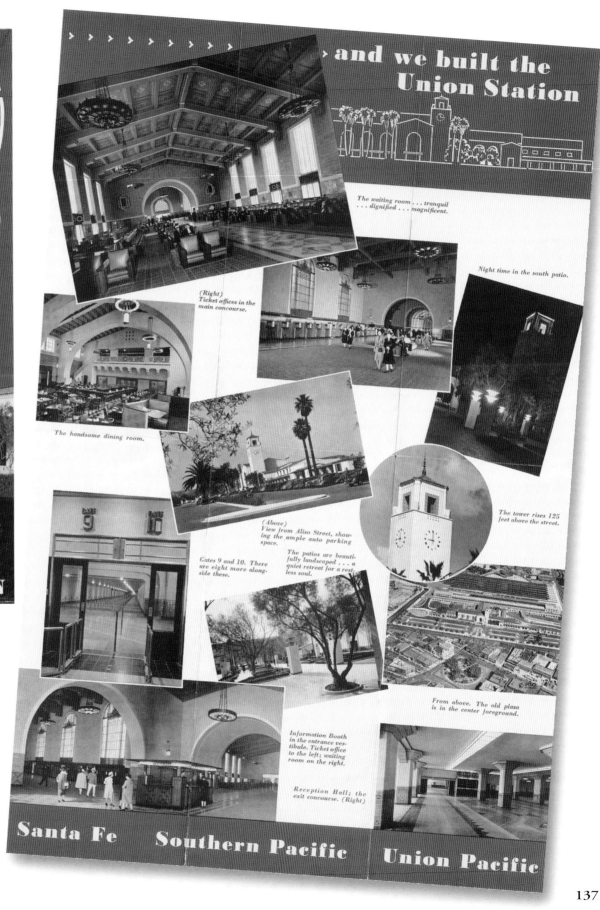

To acquaint you —

with the new

★ LOS ANGELES
★ UNION STATION

...and we built the
Union Station

The waiting room ... tranquil ... dignified ... magnificent.

Night time in the south patio.

(Right)
Ticket offices in the main concourse.

The handsome dining room.

The tower rises 125 feet above the street.

(Above)
View from Aliso Street, showing the ample auto parking space.

Gates 9 and 10. There are eight more alongside these.

The patios are beautifully landscaped ... a quiet retreat for a restless soul.

From above. The old plaza is in the center foreground.

Information Booth in the entrance vestibule. Ticket office to the left; waiting room on the right.

Reception Hall; the exit concourse. (Right)

Santa Fe　　Southern Pacific　　Union Pacific

A Santa Fe *San Diegan* (with the railroad's experimental Pendulum car tucked in ahead of the Budd-built observation) negotiates LAUPT's throat trackage circa 1947. Traffic through the station throat was controlled by operators and an interlocking plant in Terminal Tower, visible above the third-to-last car in the train. Mission Tower, which controlled mainline access, lay about a quarter-mile beyond, next to the Los Angeles River.—ROBERT O. HALE, M. D. MC CARTER COLLECTION VIA JOE WELSH

The train concourse was located at the east end of the main waiting room, and gave access to the station's 16 stub-ended passenger tracks via ten train gates and a subway passage. An additional eight tracks were allocated to mail and express traffic; five more tracks were dedicated to private-car parking and servicing; and ten tracks were used for such "administrative" purposes as car storage, locomotive access, and switching. In total, LAUPT was served by 39 tracks when it opened. The stub-end design would to a degree prove to be a bit of a nemesis to operations. At the time of its construction, it was assumed that all trains serving LAUPT would originate and terminate there. However, the Amtrak era ushered in through-train operations, the first being the extension of the Seattle–Oakland–Los Angeles train to San Diego during the summer of 1971. Later, selected *San Diegan* trains would begin operating through L.A. to points north on Southern Pacific's Coast Line. These through operations required back-up moves to access LAUPT (because of track arrangements in the L.A. area, Santa Fe's and later Amtrak's *San Diegan* runs backed in or out of the station).

The terminal was located a short distance from downtown Los Angeles, about ten minutes by car, with automobile access originally augmented by both the Los Angeles Railway and the Pacific Electric. A taxi ramp was situated off of Aliso Street, and parking spaces were provided for 625 cars (with 125 of these in an underground lot). Streetcars of the LA Railway's "N" Line entered the terminal via a loop track off of Macy Street, while the big red interurban cars of the PE ran past the opposite end of LAUPT along Aliso Street. From its downtown L.A. terminal at 6th and Main streets, the famous PE distributed travelers to hundreds of L.A.-area communities as far flung as San Bernardino and Santa Monica.

LAUPT's three "steam" railroads—Santa Fe, Union Pacific, and Southern Pacific—graced the terminal with their long-distance flagship trains as well as more mundane but equally colorful schedules. Among the station's most celebrated long-distance trains were the Santa Fe's *Chief* and *Super Chief*, Union Pacific's *City of Los Angeles* and *Challenger*, and Southern Pacific's *Daylight*s, *Lark*, and *Sunset Limited*. Some of SP's *Daylight*s were more regional in scope, as were the Santa Fe's *San Diegan*s.

LAUPT's nadir came with Amtrak's arrival on May 1, 1971, after which the station was home to only a modest cache of trains: the *Super Chief-El Capitan*, *Sunset*, a then-nameless L.A.–Oakland-Portland service (now the *Coast Starlight*), and three L.A.–San Diego round trips. From that low point, however, Los Angeles Union Passenger Terminal experienced a rebirth that would, during the remainder of the twentieth century, confirm its status as one of America's great transportation centers.

LIGHTS . . . CAMERA . . . STATION!

Given its proximity to Hollywood and its photogenic appearance, it's hardly surprising that Los Angeles Union Passenger Terminal has graced the silver screen on more than one occasion. LAUPT's roles have ranged from bit parts and anonymous backgrounds in innumerable motion pictures and television productions to a prominent role in Rudolph Mate's 1950 film-noire classic, "Union Station."

While LAUPT benefitted from being something of an honorary back-lot property, terminals in other parts of the country have also earned prominent screen time over the years. The erstwhile integration of the railroad terminal—and rail travel itself—into daily American life is reflected in film appearances where the structures are woven seamlessly into the fabric of the screenplay. How else would the idealistic Jefferson Smith—played by James Stewart in Frank Capra's "Mr. Smith Goes to Washington" (1939)—have arrived in the nation's capital but through the colonnade of Washington Union Station?

Director Alfred Hitchcock incorporated Washington Union into the opening credits of 1951's "Strangers on a Train," and stitched a trip aboard the 20th Century Limited into his 1959 thriller, "North by Northwest" (a film thankfully having outlived the working title of "The Man on Lincoln's Nose"). The British director gave audiences glimpses of both New York's Grand Central Terminal and Chicago's La Salle Street Station in all their mundane splendor. Philadelphia's 30th Street Station served as a similarly unassuming set for parts of the 1985 Harrison Ford mystery, "Witness."

Hitchcock, meanwhile, was not the only director to take advantage of Chicago's terminal menu. With railroads and "gangsters" both figuring prominently in the Windy City's popular history, the city's railroad terminals have been long-time favorites in front of the cameras. As "streamliner fever" swept a Depression-weary nation in the mid-1930s, RKO's "The Silver Streak" cast the Burlington's new Zephyr 9900 in a starring role. The stainless-steel Budd trainset made appearances at Union Stations in both Denver and

Chicago over the course of the film. This campy 1935 release is not to be confused with "Silver Streak," a 1976 action-comedy starring Gene Wilder, Richard Pryor, and Jill Clayburgh, which also included scenes filmed in Chicago Union Station as well as a brief cameo appearance of North Western Terminal's Bush train shed and even Toronto Union Station. In the case of the 1976 title, Silver Streak was the name of the cross-country train central to the plot—in this case a leased consist of Canadian Pacific Canadian Budd equipment.

Chicago Union Station has also been seen in "The Untouchables" (1987) and "The Sting" (1973), with La Salle Street Station also appearing in the latter film. Chicago's Grand Central Station even got into the act, so to speak, when scenes for the 1968 film "Gaily, Gaily" were shot under its train shed. Keep a sharp eye the next time you're in the theater or watching the late movie on television—you may catch a glimpse of an old friend, perhaps even in disguise.

In September 1986, vintage New York Central equipment once again graced Grand Central Terminal for filming of "Sullivan Street," starring Kelly McGillis and Jeff Daniels. Privately owned Budd observation car No. 48—complete with fictitious *Chicago Express* drumhead—punctuated the rear of the film consist, while two former GCT electric motors (T3a No. 278 and S1 No. 100) were brought in from their museum home at Albany, New York.—JIM BOYD

Southern Pacific GS-4 No. 4451 heads up train 59,the *West Coast*, at LAUPT circa 1950. Note the trusswork supporting the terminal's trademark platform shelters.—ROBERT O. HALE, M. D. MC CARTER COLLECTION VIA JOE WELSH

On May 5 and 6, 1989, the three railroads that built LAUPT, along with post-1971 occupant Amtrak, joined forces to celebrate the station's 50th birthday. Vintage locomotives from the terminal's colorful past—steam and diesel—were the focal point of the weekend's festivities, which also included displays of Amtrak equipment.

LAUPT's rejuvenation since 1971 has followed several paths, one of the most important occurring when it became the heart of the Southern California Regional Rail Authority's Metrolink heavy-rail commuter system, inaugurated in October 1992. By October 1995, six separate Metrolink lines were operating out of LAUPT. The station also became the terminus of the city's 17.4-mile Metro Rail Red Line (a heavy-rail subway opened in January 1993 by

the Los Angeles County Metropolitan Transportation Authority) and the light-rail Blue Line to Pasadena. In October 1995, the Gateway Center—a bus terminal, office tower, and restaurant complex—opened on LAUPT property adjacent to the terminal. Add to this Amtrak's booming *San Diegan* service—now more appropriately known as *Pacific Surfliner*s since the extension of the San Diego–L.A. corridor north to Santa Barbara and San Luis Obispo— and you have the busiest rail terminal west of Chicago.

The creators of Los Angeles Union Passenger Terminal had indeed fulfilled their ambition, as stated upon the station's opening in 1939, to "provide the people of Southern California with an institution that will serve them well for a long time to come."

TIES THAT BIND ⑦

• MONTREAL • TORONTO • HAMILTON • WINNIPEG

ABOVE: Designed by Warren & Wetmore, Winnipeg Union Station brought Beaux Arts classicism to Canada when it opened in 1911. The main entrance—photographed on May 27, 2000—presents this grand arch to travelers on the city's Broadway.
—KEVIN HOLLAND

RIGHT: Canadian National's morning *Rapido* glides east out of Toronto Union Station at the start of its high-speed, limited-stop run to Montreal in June 1968. Toronto Union Station—visible at left—today is a hub for VIA Rail Canada long-distance and regional trains, numerous GO Transit suburban runs, and the north-south operations of regional carrier Ontario Northland. The structure looming at right is the Royal York Hotel, built by the Canadian Pacific Railway and opened in 1929.
—MIKE SCHAFER

When a resident of the U.S. or Canada crosses the border between those two nations today, odds are they are traveling as a passenger in an automobile or aboard an aircraft. While the number of persons crossing the border by rail is miniscule, they continue a long and colorful tradition of international passenger service binding the two countries—a service that virtually stopped altogether when Amtrak began on May 1, 1971. Since then, new ties have been re-established, and at the dawn of a new century, international rail travel is again on the upswing.

Not coincidentally, some of Canada's best-known railway terminals figured prominently in the ebb and flow of cross-border passenger traffic, serving as northern anchors for international routes operated by U.S. railroads, sometimes jointly with Canadian carriers. Canada's terminals also mirrored U.S. travel patterns in that they served as gateways for Canadians traveling about the provinces or from coast to coast aboard the Canadian Pacific Railway, Canadian National Railways, on one of Canada's regional railroads, or on VIA Rail—today Canada's principal rail passenger operator.

142

MONTREAL
Windsor Station

The Canadian Pacific Railway is inexorably linked with the history of Canada. It was the CPR, after all, that brought west and east together in 1885, promoting the new nation and transported immigrants, settlers, and tourists through the balance of the nineteenth and well into the twentieth centuries. As well, CP forged enduring ties to Europe and Asia through its steamship and airline subsidiaries.

Until Canadian Pacific's head office moved to Calgary, Alberta, in 1996, Montreal had been the company's only home. Windsor Station, the CPR's combined Montreal headquarters and passenger terminal, was as fitting a structure as could be imagined to host the CPR and its transcontinental and regional passenger trains. The Richardsonian Romanesque station's baronial overtones evoked the stolid character of the line's Scottish founders, Donald A. Smith (Baron Strathcona) and his cousin George Stephen (Baron Mount Stephen). The CPR's first general manager, and the line's president after 1888, was William Cornelius Van Horne, and Windsor Station was very much a product of his vision.

Van Horne awarded the commission for the station's design to New York architect Bruce Price (1845–1902), who also happened to be the father of etiquette columnist Emily Post. In 1886, Van Horne had assigned Price the task of designing the railway's first Banff Springs Hotel, and in 1891, obviously satisfied with the architect's work, awarded him the commission for the CPR's Chateau Frontenac Hotel in Quebec City.

FACING PAGE: Headquarters of "the World's Greatest Transportation System," CPR's Windsor Station was notable as one of the first examples of Richardsonian Romanesque architecture in Canada. This August 1956 view looks down Windsor Street. Bruce Price's original structure is closest to the camera, with the office and tower block farther along Windsor Street added between 1910 and 1915.—JIM SHAUGHNESSY

UPPER LEFT: Another August 1956 view shows Windsor Station's "Maxwell Wing," an addition built along Osborne Street between 1900 and 1906.—JIM SHAUGHNESSY

BELOW: This is the *Viger* leaving Windsor Station for Quebec City in June 1968. The arch-windowed skyscraper is the Canadian Pacific's Chateau Champlain Hotel, opened the previous year.—MIKE SCHAFER

Obviously inspired by the work of Henry Hobson Richardson (1838–1886), Price created for the CPR's Windsor Station a massive, turreted structure faced in rusticated limestone that introduced the Richardsonian Romanesque style to Canada in a massive and entirely appropriate manner. Construction began at the corner of Windsor Street and what was then Osborne Street (today's Rue de la Gauchetiere) in June 1887.

Barely a decade after Windsor Station's February 1889 opening—marked in part by a six-foot-tall banner which read, "Beats All Creation—The New CPR Station"—the terminal was enlarged between 1900 and 1906. A new north facade with a low porte-cochere—dubbed the "Maxwell Wing" in honor of its architect, Edward Maxwell—blended imperceptibly with the original structure, as did a 14-story office expansion and tower erected at the original station's south end between 1910 and 1915. This major addition was a cooperative effort of three architects—J. W. H. Watts (1850–1917), L. F. Taylor (1850– 1917), and W. S. Painter (1877–1957). Between 1905 and 1911, Walter Painter served as Canadian Pacific's first chief architect.

Windsor Station's airy concourse, dating to 1915, was photographed in August 1956. This view looks south, with train gates   and the terminal's elaborate brass indicator board visible at right.—JIM SHAUGHNESSY

CPR Pacific No. 1261 steamed under Windsor Station's Bush train shed on November 25, 1955. In later years, tracks under the shed were removed, with passengers forced to endure a long walk to and from their trains. This view illustrates how the Bush shed was designed to maximize shelter to passengers and equipment while at the same time providing an efficient outlet for locomotive exhaust. Those parts of the structure directly exposed to the exhaust blast were encased in concrete to minimize corrosion damage. While not perfect, the Bush design and others like it were improvements over earlier "balloon" sheds.—JIM SHAUGHNESSY

The 1910–1915 work also resulted in expansion of the train shed, a large new waiting room, and an airy glass- and steel-lattice-capped passenger concourse. Locomotive and passenger-car servicing and coach yard facilities were provided a short distance west at Glen Yard, adjacent to the railway's Montreal West suburban station.

Service to the U.S. was provided by the CPR in conjunction with international service partners New York Central, Delaware & Hudson, and Boston & Maine. The result, particularly in the postwar "lightweight" years, was an eclectic mix of rolling stock and locomotives that enlivened the omnipresent palette of CPR maroon.

Two minor additions were made to Windsor Station: in 1953 an express wing was built along the north side of the train shed, and in 1954 a telecommunications wing was added on the south side of the property abutting St. Antoine Street. Structural changes made thereafter were retrenchments, the most drastic of which saw much of the train shed removed by CP Rail (Canadian Pacific's post-1968 designation for its railroad) in the early 1970s and the track cut back, requiring passengers to take a longer hike between train and headhouse.

International services to and from Windsor Station endured a three-year hiatus from the May 1971 demise of the D&H's Montreal–New York *Laurentian* and *Montreal Limited* until Amtrak and the State of New York inaugurated the *Adirondack* over the same route in August 1974. Windsor Station remained an important Canadian intercity terminal through this period, even after responsibility

The *Dominion* is about to depart on its transcontinental trek to Vancouver on November 25, 1955, with *Kokanee Park's* streamlined Budd features in gleaming contrast to the confines of Windsor Station's train shed.—JIM SHAUGHNESSY

for CP Rail's passenger operations had been assumed by VIA Rail Canada in October 1978.

VIA, in many ways Amtrak's northern counterpart as the newly created operator of most of Canada's intercity passenger trains, was hard-pressed to justify a need for two

Boston & Maine E7A No. 3807 leads an all-CPR consist as the jointly operated *Alouette* departs Montreal for Boston in this early 1950s view. The 14-story tower of Windsor Station's 1910-1915 expansion is visible above the rear car.—CANADIAN PACIFIC; KEVIN HOLLAND COLLECTION

147

C.N.R STATION.

This is how Montreal's Central Station looked before the air-rights developments of Place Ville Marie, the Queen Elizabeth Hotel, and Place Bonaventure virtually obscured it from the streetscape after 1958. This view looks southwest across University Avenue.—PATERSON-GEORGE COLLECTION

Montreal stations. VIA's Montreal schedules were consolidated at nearby Central Station, while Windsor survives as a commuter terminal serving Montreal's western suburbs.

CENTRAL STATION

Central Station was the Canadian National Railway's somewhat spartan terminal located at the south end of the double-track, 16,315-foot Mount Royal Tunnel. Central Station officially opened on July 14, 1943, to replace the adjacent stub-ended Tunnel Station which closed the previous day. Construction of Tunnel Station, and the $12-million tunnel itself, had been undertaken in 1911 by CNR predecessor Canadian Northern (CNoR) to give its trains access to downtown Montreal from the west. With the Canadian Pacific and Grand Trunk already occupying the logical western approaches between the St. Lawrence River and Mount Royal's imposing 769-foot mass, the Johnny-come-lately CNoR had little option but to go *through* the mountain instead of around it. The railway

made the best of the situation, however, farsightedly acquiring nearly 5,000 acres of land adjacent to the new tunnel's north portal to establish a planned residential community served by the railway's suburban trains. The CNoR was able to recoup the cost of the tunnel through the sale of real estate in the town of Mount Royal.

The long tunnel made the hauling of occupied passenger cars behind steam locomotives problematic, as there existed the very real risk of asphyxiation in addition to the lesser nuisances of soot and cinders. The problem was solved with the introduction of Canada's most ambitious trunk-line electrification, with boxcab-design electric motors (later augmented by center-cab designs) employed to pull passenger trains through the tunnel. Intercity trains swapped electric power for steam locomotives north of the tunnel, while suburban multiple-unit and motor-hauled trains continued under wire to the city's western reaches.

Central Station's virtually unadorned style, the work of architect John Schofield, was as much a function of contemporary design trends as it was of wartime austerity. Although construction began in 1938, Canada had been at war for almost four years when the new station opened, and if any North American passenger terminal could claim a baptism by fire, it was Central. Not only did the facility assume the traffic of the cramped five-track Tunnel Station which it directly replaced, but most of the passenger services hitherto handled at the CNR's Bonaventure Station (a former Grand Trunk facility) also moved into Central.

Of Central Station's 18 tracks, all but two were used for passenger access. The remaining pair was devoted to express traffic. To accommodate those trains previously routed to nearby Bonaventure Station, an earth-and-concrete

viaduct was built leading south from the new station toward the St. Lawrence River. Near the river, the tracks curved west past the railway's sprawling Pointe St. Charles shops and connected with existing CNR routes to Ontario, the West, and—via the multiple-truss Victoria Bridge—to eastern Quebec, the Maritime provinces, and the Eastern U.S.

In addition to the trains of owner Canadian National, Central Station hosted schedules operated by two of CNR's U.S. subsidiaries. Central Vermont's overnight *Montrealer* and *Washingtonian*, operated in conjunction with the Boston & Maine, New Haven, and Pennsylvania railroads, conveyed through cars to New York City and Washington, D.C., until September 1966; these trains were reincarnated by Amtrak in October 1972. The CV also operated daylight services between Montreal, Boston, and New York while CNR family affiliate Grand Trunk (not to be confused with corporate sibling Grand Trunk Western serving Chicago) scheduled a Montreal–Portland, Maine, service that was cut back and eventually disappeared as a summer weekend-only train in the early 1960s. Prior to 1953, Central Station also hosted a New York City–Montreal through service operated by the CNR in conjunction with New York Central and the fabled Rutland Railroad.

Within Central Station itself, Schofield combined the traditional great hall, ticket areas, waiting room, concourse, and gates into a single open space located directly above the electrified platform tracks. Steam locomotives were prohibited from the station for the same reason they had been banned from the tunnel. Escalators and fixed stairs led passengers to and from their trains.

Architect John Schofield merged the traditionally disparate terminal functions of great hall, baggage and ticketing areas, waiting room, concourse, and train gates in his design for Montreal's Central Station. Visible in this 1969 view are Sebastiano Oiello's bas-relief murals, notable in a terminal featuring little in the way of ornamentation.—JIM HEUER

Central Station's international flavor was illustrated in January 1980, as Amtrak's arriving *Montrealer* from Washington, D.C., and New York City passed a former Canadian National FPA-4 preparing to depart with its VIA schedule for Toronto. Place Bonaventure, built above the tracks immediately south of the station, looms over the VIA cab-unit. Central Station was an oddity among Canadian terminals with its high-level platforms, which let passengers enter and exit trains at car-floor height.
—KEVIN HOLLAND

Already a largely subterranean station, Central virtually disappeared from Montreal's streetscape after 1958 when the Place Ville Marie skyscraper complex and other developments took advantage of the railway's air rights between the tunnel's south portal and the station. Central's vanishing act was made even more complete when the 1964 Place Bonaventure monolith straddled the station's southern tracks.

Central survives, however, fulfilling its original utilitarian purpose. It became a hub of activity within Montreal's "underground city" of interconnected retail tunnels and subway stations, and included traffic surges brought on by a World's Fair (1967) and an Olympic Games (1976) in its resume.

With the consolidation of VIA Rail Canada's intercity trains from nearby Windsor Station in 1984, followed by Amtrak's *Adirondack* in 1986, Central became Montreal's only active intercity terminal. While Amtrak's *Montrealer* no longer runs, the New York-Montreal *Adirondack* maintains Central's status as an international anchor.

TORONTO UNION STATION

The largest passenger terminal in Canada traces its origins to a catastrophic April 1904 fire which, while sparing the old Union Station, nonetheless managed to clear a prime parcel of city-owned waterfront land perfectly suited for a much-needed replacement terminal.

In 1905, the Canadian Pacific and the Grand Trunk railways formally set the replacement process in motion, but it would be a staggering and frustrating 25 years before the new Toronto Union Station would be occupied and fully operational. In the interim, the Grand Trunk would cease to exist, having become part of the government-controlled Canadian National Railways system in 1923.

After haggling over project details for years, the CPR and GTR announced their choice of architects for the new station in 1913. The GTR selected George A. Ross (1879–1946) and Robert H. MacDonald (1875–1942), partners from Montreal. The CPR chose Hugh G. Jones (1872–1947), also based in Montreal, while John M. Lyle (1872–1945) was a Torontonian. The group worked quickly, with drawings complete and initial construction work underway by September 1914—just weeks after war had broken out in Europe.

Wartime shortages of manpower and materials meant that the station's basic headhouse structure was not completed until 1918. Following two more years of interior finishing, the station's railway offices and postal facilities were ready for occupancy in 1920.

Another seven years were to pass, however, before Toronto Union Station was ready for passengers, and even then only haphazardly. A massive grade-separation project, involving an earth-and-concrete viaduct and several bridges and underpasses, was required to elevate trackage to the level dictated by the new station's proposed concourse and platform arrangement.

A Phoenix quite literally risen from the ashes, Toronto Union Station was erected on land cleared by a disastrous 1904 fire. The largest railway terminal in Canada, Union Station's Beaux Arts facade stretches for over 750 feet along Front Street. This June 1978 view looks southeast from the corner of York Street. Early plans called for Union Station to be the southern anchor of a monumental boulevard of the sort espoused by the City Beautiful Movement, but this never came to pass.—MIKE SCHAFER

With the CPR's new Royal York Hotel as a backdrop, one of the railway's Pacifics heads up a Montreal-bound train on the east side of Toronto Union Station circa 1931.
—DAVE SHAW COLLECTION

The station was officially opened by the Prince of Wales (later—briefly—King Edward VIII)—who happened to be on a visit to Canada—on August 6, 1927. By August 11, railway operations had been transferred from the adjacent old station, and the new Toronto Union Station was opened to the public. Alas, construction of the through platform trackage and ten-track, 1,200-foot-long Bush train shed was far from complete, impeded in part by interference from portions of the old station then being demolished. These elements of the new facility would not be in full use until December 15, 1930. The entire terminal facility was deemed officially complete on September 1, 1931—over 27 years after the fire.

The station's Beaux Arts head house, with its nearly 800-foot frontage and imposing entrance colonnade, bore a somewhat economical resemblance to New York's Pennsylvania Station. The head house's exterior was faced with Indiana limestone. Occupying the block south of Front Street between York and Bay streets, the west wing housed railway offices while a corresponding east wing was built as a postal facility. Inside the 260-foot x 86-foot x 88-foot-high Great Hall, a soaring arch of Guastavino tile comprised the coffered ceiling, while the floors were laid with gray and pink Tennessee marble and the walls faced with beige Zumbro stone. Four-story-tall arched windows, into which walkways were incorporated to connect the station's office areas, framed the east and west ends of the room.

As built, the station was noted for its efficient separation of arriving and departing passenger flow, an arrangement essentially unchanged until the debut of GO Transit commuter service in May 1967. GO, the name of which is an acronym for the Government of Ontario, was originally allotted station tracks 2 and 3 along with station facilities in what had until then been the lower (arrivals) concourse, essentially creating a "station within a station."

By 1980, the success and expansion of GO commuter services led to redevelopment of former postal space in the station's east basement into a much larger self-contained commuter terminal. The station's original arrivals area once again was dedicated to intercity passengers.

In the interim, VIA Rail Canada had taken over responsibility for the operation of former Canadian National and Canadian Pacific passenger trains. By October 1978, when former CP services were fully integrated, VIA became the terminal's major intercity presence. The status of a "union" station remained, however, by virtue of trains operated by the Ontario Northland Railway (which reached Toronto over CN trackage south of North Bay), and, after 1981, Amtrak.

Amtrak's trains to New York City (the *Maple Leaf*) and Chicago (the *International*) are a legacy of the cross-border trains and through cars formerly operated into Union Station by the CNR and CPR in conjunction with the New York Central, Grand Trunk Western, and Lehigh Valley railroads.

When CN and CP announced their proposed Metro Centre redevelopment of Toronto's downtown rail lands in December 1968, they set in motion three decades of urban renewal which, early on, very nearly cost Toronto its Union Station. While notable elements of the original plan were in fact implemented—such as the city's landmark CN Tower, a major convention center, and a long-sought headquarters for the Canadian Broadcasting Corporation—public outcry saved Union Station from destruction. The terminal remains a vital part of Toronto's transportation infrastructure, serving as an interface between intercity,

ABOVE: Toronto Union Station's Great Hall as it appeared in the spring of 1978. Staircases at both ends of the vast room led down to the station's arrivals level, which hosted GO Transit ticketing functions by the time of this view. Departing intercity passengers reached their underground concourse through the colonnade at right. Ticket windows line the wall at left.
—MIKE SCHAFER

RIGHT: From TurboTrains to LRC's, Toronto Union Station has played host to some of North America's most innovative—if not always completely successful—rail-travel developments. Among the most successful were the commuter trains originally operated by CN for the Government of Ontario and introduced in May 1967. An early "GO" train pauses beneath Union Station's Bush train shed in June 1968, en route through the station to Pickering in Toronto's eastern suburbs.—MIKE SCHAFER

commuter, and subway trains, as well as an important link in the city's all-weather network of pedestrian tunnels, one of which leads to the nearby famous Royal York Hotel, once a CPR property.

HAMILTON, ONTARIO

The Toronto, Hamilton & Buffalo Railway was, for most of its existence, the jointly owned corporate child of the New York Central and the Canadian Pacific. The TH&B served, to paraphrase its own slogan, as a vital link between these "two great systems."

In the days before DC-3s, Convair 240s, Viscounts, and their airborne descendants made short order of business travel between Toronto and the likes of New York,

Boston, Pittsburgh, Cleveland, and Upstate New York, the New York Central enjoyed a respectable passenger trade between those points.

The TH&B figured prominently in the equation, conveying the trains and through sleeping cars of its parent railroads between Buffalo's Central Terminal, where connection was made with New York Central, and Hamilton, Ontario, where Canadian Pacific took over to forward consists to and from Toronto's Union Station via Canadian National trackage rights.

In addition to its importance as a connection in the three-way pool service, Hamilton—an important industrial and manufacturing center at the western tip of Lake Ontario—was the location of the TH&B's headquarters.

BELOW LEFT: In 1975, the CN Tower became the tallest freestanding structure in the world, part of a redevelopment of railway lands that nearly cost Toronto its Union Station. In July 1979, a westbound VIA train negotiated trackage near Bathurst Street.—KEVIN HOLLAND

BELOW: The CN Tower provided the vantage point for this May 1976 view of CN's Spadina Avenue engine terminal and coach yard. Today, the Skydome stadium occupies the former engine terminal site.—KEVIN HOLLAND

The TH&B Railway's Hunter Street Station is regarded as the first example of International Style architecture in Canada. A semi-circular marquee—visible at right—denoted the building's main entrance. Photographed on August 9, 1978, the Hunter Street Station survives as a multimodal commuter terminal.—KEVIN HOLLAND

This was reason enough, the parties decided, to erect a combined passenger terminal and office tower to replace the TH&B's outmoded 1895 station and at the same time accede to long-standing civic demands for a grade-separated right-of-way through the city core.

The project was undertaken at the onset of the Great Depression by no less an architectural firm than NYC's favored Fellheimer & Wagner, fresh from their Buffalo Central Terminal commission. They produced a vest-pocket terminal in the International Style that was just coming into vogue—marked by a streamlined simplicity, yet with geometric echoes of the slightly earlier high Art Deco style. In fact, Fellheimer & Wagner's original May 1930 Hamilton project drawings had depicted a decidedly Art Deco structure, with setbacks and a strong verticality calling to mind a scaled-down version of Buffalo's new landmark.

Hunter Street Station, as the Hamilton facility came to be known, opened to passenger traffic in 1933 and served Toronto–Buffalo through traffic until 1981. In both the steam and diesel era, locomotives and passenger cars of all three railroads were common sights at Hunter Street. Conventional locomotive-hauled trains were replaced in 1970 by Canadian Pacific Rail Diesel Cars (RDCs), with the last through-sleepers offered by NYC successor Penn Central having been discontinued in September of that year. The RDC service—just one round-trip each day—survived the coming of Amtrak by remaining a Canadian operation, initially under CP Rail and, after 1978, as a ward of VIA Rail Canada. When Amtrak and VIA cooperated to launch a direct Toronto–New York City day train in 1981, the new run's routing over Canadian National between Hamilton and the border crossing at Niagara Falls brought an end to Hunter Street's career as an intercity passenger terminal. (The new Amtrak-VIA *Maple Leaf's* Hamilton stop was at the 1930 CNR station near the city's harbor.)

During a decade of dormancy the TH&B itself was absorbed by CP Rail and disappeared as a corporate entity and various schemes were advanced to redevelop Hunter Street Station. Finally, in the mid-1990s, the facility emerged as a multimodal commuter terminal—ideally situated in the city's downtown core—accommodating expanded GO Transit rail service from Toronto. In a reversal of fortune, these GO schedules were shifted from Hamilton's former CNR station, which also lost its status as a VIA stop in favor of a newly built (and even-more-isolated) structure adjacent to a suburban expressway.

WINNIPEG

This prairie city is very much the crossroads of Canadian railroading, a vital link between east and west and a community entwined with its railroads. Both of Canada's transcontinental main lines pass through Winnipeg, and the city was an early beneficiary of significant yard and repair shop installations. Winnipeg's proximity to the U.S. border encouraged a north-south influx to Canada's predominantly east-west flow of commerce, and the volume of passenger traffic passing through the city mandated that appropriate facilities be built to care for the trains and their passengers.

Union Station

Winnipeg Union Station was built between 1908 and 1911 for the Grand Trunk Pacific and Canadian Northern railways, whose managers envisioned a facility that would overshadow the existing CPR station just north of downtown. The Beaux Arts station that resulted from this rivalry has strong ties to another classic passenger terminal. Winnipeg Union Station was designed by Warren & Wetmore, the New York firm whose other major project at the time was their fractious collaboration with Reed & Stem on New York's Grand Central Terminal.

The CNoR and GTP became major components of the Canadian National Railways system (CNR) in 1923, yet Winnipeg remained a "union" station for decades by virtue of the Great Northern and Northern Pacific passenger trains that crossed the international border on their treks from the Twin Cities and intermediate points until the coming of Amtrak in 1971.

The 350 x 140-foot, four-story headhouse terminated the city's Broadway at the intersection of Main Street. Upon passing through a vestibule from Main Street, passengers entered an 88-foot-diameter, 93-foot-high rotunda which served as the station's ticket lobby. On the north side of this domed room was the main waiting room, along with a restaurant, lunch room, and separate mens' and ladies' waiting rooms. Various offices, baggage, and mail facilities were located on the opposite side.

Winnipeg Union Station survives as both a museum and a functional passenger facility. Train shed tracks 1 and 2 contain displays of historic railway equipment, while VIA Rail Canada's *Canadian* and *Hudson Bay* still call at the station on their semi-weekly schedules. The former sprawling railway freight and express terminals to the station's east have been redeveloped into The Forks, a mixed-use entertainment and dining attraction bordering the Red and Assiniboine Rivers.

LEFT: Winnipeg Union Station's soaring rotunda as it appeared in the spring of 1977.—MIKE SCHAFER

BELOW: The rotunda's dome is just visible in this 1977 exterior view of Canadian National's Winnipeg Station. The boxy structure supporting the "CN" signs was not part of Warren & Wetmore's original design. The starkness of the station was deliberate, on the direction of CN predecessor Canadian Northern. The CNoR sought an efficient, unpretentious facility.—MIKE SCHAFER

INDEX